LSAT®

PrepTest 81

Unlocked

Exclusive Data, Analysis, & Explanations for the June 2017 LSAT

PUBLISHING

New York

© 2017 by Kaplan, Inc.

Published by Kaplan Publishing, a division of Kaplan, Inc.
750 Third Avenue
New York, NY 10017

ISBN: 978-1-5062-2341-4
10 9 8 7 6 5 4 3 2 1

The Inside Story

PrepTest 81 was administered in June 2017. It challenged 27,606 test takers. What made this test so hard? Here's a breakdown of what Kaplan students who were surveyed after taking the official exam considered PrepTest 81's most difficult section.

Hardest PrepTest 81 Section as Reported by Test Takers

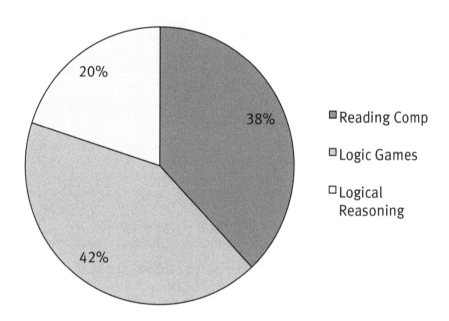

20%
38%
42%

■ Reading Comp

□ Logic Games

□ Logical Reasoning

Based on these results, you might think that studying Logic Games is the key to LSAT success. Well, Logic Games is important, but test takers' perceptions don't tell the whole story. For that, you need to consider students' actual performance. Alas, PrepTest 81 is so recent that as of the time of publication we don't yet have sufficient data about student performance on this test. ***Your online materials will be updated to reflect performance data later in the fall of 2017.***

Actual student performance typically tells quite a different story. Usually students are fairly equally likely to miss questions in all three of the different section types.

Maybe students overestimate the difficulty of the Logic Games section because it's so unusual, or maybe it's because a really hard logic game is so easy to remember after the test. But the truth is that the testmaker places hard questions throughout the test. When we update the information in fall of 2017, we'll include the locations of the 10 hardest (most missed) questions in the exam.

To maximize your potential on the LSAT, you need to take a comprehensive approach. Test yourself rigorously, and review your performance on every section of the test. Kaplan's LSAT explanations provide the expertise and insight you need to fully understand your results. The explanations are written and edited by a team of LSAT experts, who have helped thousands of students improve their scores. Kaplan always provides data-driven analysis of the test, ranking the difficulty of every question based on actual student performance. The ten hardest questions on every test are highlighted with a 4-star difficulty rating, the highest we give. The analysis breaks down the remaining questions into 1-, 2-, and 3-star ratings so that you can compare your performance to thousands of other test takers on all LSAC material. ***As soon as we get sufficient data, we'll update the star ratings for PrepTest 81 in fall of 2017.***

7 Can't Miss Features of PrepTest 81

- With 10 Inference questions in LR, PT 81 had the most Inference questions since December '94 (PT 13).
- The Logic Games section has only started with a Hybrid game nine times ever. That said, PT 81 was the third test in three years to do so.
- PT 81's Reading Comprehension section contained only two Global questions. That ties June '16 (PT 78) as the fewest ever.
- What replaced those Global questions? There were four LR - Parallel Reasoning questions in the RC section. That's a new record, and equals the same number there were on PT 77–80 combined!
- (D)-lightful! There were at least two more (D)'s than (C)'s or (E)'s in all three sections!
- A/B Testing? The second LR section had some pretty unusual letter answer streaks. #7 to #15 were all either (A) or (B)—including four straight (B)'s in one stretch.
- Dangerous Curve Ahead! PT 81 was the first test since October '08 (PT 58) to require at least 83 questions correct to get a 164 (90th percentile score). Similarly, PT 81 was the first test since June '07 (PT June '07) to require at least 94 questions correct to get a 172 (99th percentile score).

PrepTest 81 in Context

As much fun as it is to find out what makes a PrepTest unique or noteworthy, it's even more important to know just how representative it is of other LSAT administrations (and, thus, how likely it is to be representative of the exam you will face on Test Day). The following charts compare the numbers of each kind of question and game on PrepTest 81 to the average numbers seen on all officially released LSATs administered over the past five years (from 2012 through 2016).

Number of LR Questions by Type: PrepTest 81 vs. 2012–2016 Average

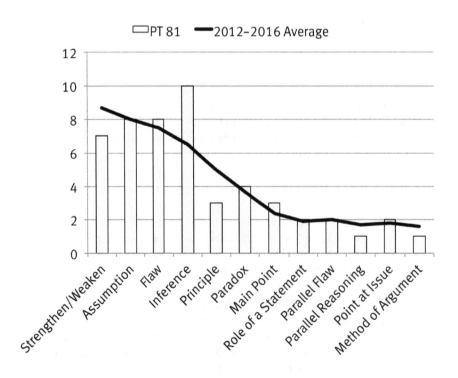

Number of LG Games by Type: PrepTest 81 vs. 2012–2016 Average

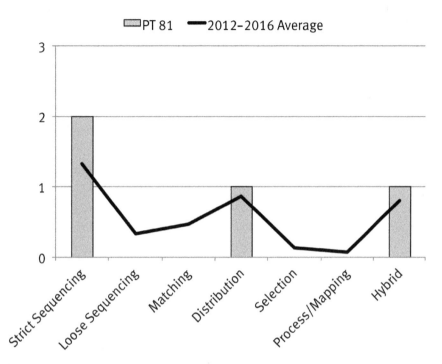

Number of RC Questions by Type: PrepTest 81 vs. 2012–2016 Average

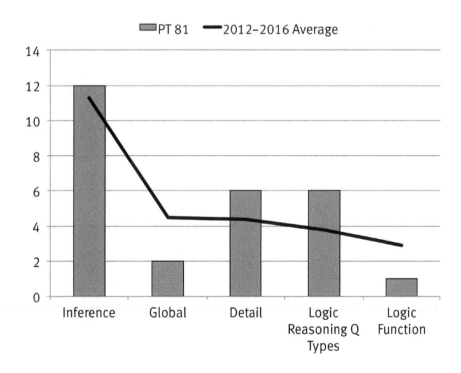

There isn't usually a huge difference in the distribution of questions from LSAT to LSAT, but if this test seems harder (or easier) to you than another you've taken, compare the number of questions of the types on which you, personally, are strongest and weakest. And then, explore within each section to see if your best or worst question types came earlier or later.

Students in Kaplan's comprehensive LSAT courses have access to every released LSAT, and to an online Qbank with thousands of officially released questions, games, and passages. If you are studying on your own, you have to do a bit more work to identify your strengths and your areas of opportunity. Quantitative analysis (like that in the previous charts) is an important tool for understanding how the test is constructed, and how you are performing on it.

Section I: Reading Comprehension
Passage 1: Wynton Marsalis and the State of Jazz

Q#	Question Type	Correct	Difficulty
1	Global	D	Check your online resources.
2	Inference	C	Check your online resources.
3	Inference	D	Check your online resources.
4	Logic Reasoning (Parallel Reasoning)	B	Check your online resources.
5	Detail	E	Check your online resources.
6	Inference	A	Check your online resources.
7	Detail	E	Check your online resources.

Passage 2: Inferential vs. Noninferential Thoughts

Q#	Question Type	Correct	Difficulty
8	Global	B	Check your online resources.
9	Logic Reasoning (Weaken)	C	Check your online resources.
10	Inference	E	Check your online resources.
11	Logic Reasoning (Parallel Reasoning)	A	Check your online resources.
12	Detail	D	Check your online resources.
13	Detail	C	Check your online resources.
14	Inference	D	Check your online resources.

Passage 3: Dowsing

Q#	Question Type	Correct	Difficulty
15	Logic Function	C	Check your online resources.
16	Detail	A	Check your online resources.
17	Logic Reasoning (Parallel Reasoning)	D	Check your online resources.
18	Inference	B	Check your online resources.
19	Detail	D	Check your online resources.
20	Inference	E	Check your online resources.

Passage 4: The Use of Independent Research by Judges

Q#	Question Type	Correct	Difficulty
21	Logic Reasoning (Principle)	C	Check your online resources.
22	Inference	A	Check your online resources.
23	Inference	D	Check your online resources.
24	Inference	B	Check your online resources.
25	Inference	C	Check your online resources.
26	Logic Reasoning (Parallel Reasoning)	B	Check your online resources.
27	Inference	D	Check your online resources.

Passage 1: Wynton Marsalis and the State of Jazz

Step 1: Read the Passage Strategically
Sample Roadmap

line #	Keyword/phrase	¶ Margin notes
3	persuasive advocacy	
4	ruled	
5	unqualified admiration	
6	unsurpassed influence	Marsalis praised
7	But	
8	increasing fire	
10	uncertain; as does	Future of Marsalis & jazz uncertain
14	In fact	After 1999, Marsalis stopped
19	drastically reduced	
20	shifting its emphasis	Columbia shift from new jazz to old
23	essentially gave up	
24	grim	
26	accused of; partly	Critics blame Marsalis
27	culpable; charge	
28	unbending; sanctifying	
30	stifling	Marsalis too traditional
31	inhibited	
33	noted	
37	Indeed	
39	great	
40	emphasis; Still; never advocated	Auth: Marsalis traditional yet innovative
41	mere	
45	However	
46	different; :	But, record execs say don't need new jazz
48	?; So	
49	shifted	
55	irresistible; :	Record companies make $ selling old jazz
56	far more profitable	
57	than	

Discussion

In the first paragraph, the author introduces a startling contrast: Jazz musician Wynton Marsalis (**Topic**) was widely praised for decades, gaining "unqualified admiration" and having "unsurpassed influence." *But* that changed, as criticism toward Marsalis led to an uncertain fate for both him and jazz music, in general.

The second paragraph goes into detail about the deterioration of both Marsalis's career and jazz. After a massive output (15 CDs in one year), Marsalis went years without releasing new music. He no longer had a record contract, and record companies stopped developing new jazz artists. It makes the reader wonder, what happened to Marsalis's sterling reputation, and how did this affect jazz as a whole? These questions serve as the **Scope** of the passage. And the **Purpose** is to answer those questions and explain what happened.

The third paragraph starts to offer some explanation, presenting the point of view of Marsalis's critics. They partially blame Marsalis for his *unbending* and *stifling* reliance on classicism, which impeded innovation.

The author defends Marsalis some in the fourth paragraph, admitting to Marsalis's emphasis on tradition, but arguing that Marsalis was using that tradition as inspiration for reinvention and expression. *However*, record companies took a different view: If traditional music is so great, then who needs new music?

And that leads to the ultimate effect described in the last paragraph: Record companies stopped pushing new artists and instead focused on making lots of money selling archived recordings of older artists. This wraps up the **Main Idea** of the passage: Despite his initial success, Marsalis's emphasis on traditional jazz styles ultimately hurt his career and led the music industry to stop supporting new jazz musicians.

1. (D) Global

Step 2: Identify the Question Type
The question asks for the "main point" of the entire passage, making this a Global question.

Step 3: Research the Relevant Text
Don't go back into the passage. Just consider the Main Idea as predicted after reading the passage.

Step 4: Make a Prediction
The Main Idea was that, despite his initial success, Marsalis's emphasis on traditional jazz hurt his career and ultimately led record companies to abandon their support for new jazz musicians.

Step 5: Evaluate the Answer Choices

(D) offers an accurate summary, bringing up Marsalis's emphasis on tradition and how that led to decreased support for new jazz artists.

(A) focuses too much on Marsalis, completely ignoring the effect on jazz music in general.

(B) addresses the author's defense of Marsalis in the fourth paragraph. However, this not only misses the point of the passage as a whole, but it also suggests that jazz now has a wider audience—a claim not supported anywhere in the passage.

(C) is a Distortion. It is never suggested that Marsalis ever moved away from traditionalism. And, if anything, the passage suggests that Marsalis's style caused the record companies to shift their focus, not the other way around.

(E) is far too narrow, focusing merely on what is mentioned in the first paragraph. However, this completely leaves out the effects described throughout the rest of the passage.

2. (C) Inference

Step 2: Identify the Question Type
The question asks what someone "most likely means" when making a claim, making this an Inference question.

Step 3: Research the Relevant Text
The quote in question is presented at the end of the third paragraph. Don't just focus on the quote itself. Consider how it relates to the point of the paragraph as a whole.

Step 4: Make a Prediction
In saying Marsalis has a "retro ideology," the executive also claims that Marsalis's ideas were more "museumlike in nature, a look back." This fits the criticism throughout the paragraph that Marsalis was *unbending* in his focus on classicism and was *stifling* in its orthodoxy. In short, the executive is suggesting that Marsalis was too caught up in the past.

Step 5: Evaluate the Answer Choices

(C) correctly identifies the idea that Marsalis was too focused on tradition.

(A) is a Distortion. Marsalis is reviving traditional ideas, but there is no suggestion that these ideas were ever *discredited*.

(B) is a Faulty Use of Detail. The author references Marsalis recombining ideas in the fourth paragraph (line 43), but this is not related to the executive's claim, which is more about Marsalis's ideas being outdated (*museumlike*).

(D) is also a Faulty Use of Detail, and a 180. It's the author who praises Marsalis for reinvention and reinterpretation (lines 41–44), not the executive. The executive is more critical and sees Marsalis as stuck in the past, rather than being inventive.

(E) is a Distortion. There is no suggestion that the ideas Marsalis used were in any way *inauthentic*.

3. (D) Inference

Step 2: Identify the Question Type
The question asks about what the author would "most likely" believe, which means the correct answer won't be directly stated, but it will be directly supported. That makes this an Inference question.

Step 3: Research the Relevant Text
The question stem refers to the "state of affairs in jazz," a phrase that (not coincidentally) appears word for word in line 24. The phrase "this grim state of affairs" indicates the author is referring to the scenario described immediately beforehand, in the second paragraph.

Step 4: Make a Prediction
The *grim* situation is that record companies have "reduced [their] roster of active jazz musicians," emphasized "reissues of old recordings," and "essentially gave up on developing new artists." That suggests the author would be much happier if record companies starting focusing on new jazz musicians again.

Step 5: Evaluate the Answer Choices

(D) is supported, as it would perfectly address the de-emphasis on new artists.

(A) is a Distortion. The author would certainly appreciate this, especially given the defense of Marsalis presented in the fourth paragraph. However, the question asks about what would make the author less negative about the state of affairs in jazz music in general, not in the treatment of Marsalis personally.

(B) is too focused on reviving Marsalis's career rather than improving the "state of affairs in jazz," as the question asks.

(C) is also too focused on defending Marsalis personally, rather than addressing the state of affairs in jazz overall.

(E) is a Distortion. The author does not have a problem with young jazz musicians. The problem is with the record companies, who are basically abandoning new jazz musicians.

4. (B) Logic Reasoning (Parallel Reasoning)

Step 2: Identify the Question Type
The question asks for a situation that is "most analogous" to one described in the passage. That makes this a Logic Reasoning question, specifically one that mimics a Parallel Reasoning question.

Step 3: Research the Relevant Text
The situation facing Marsalis is described throughout the entire passage. Use the margin notes to stay focused on the major themes, rather than getting caught up in the details.

Step 4: Make a Prediction
As described throughout the passage, Marsalis is criticized for focusing too much on traditional ideas, and this has led music companies to abandon new musicians in favor of selling older recordings. The correct answer will mimic this idea of how one's focus on tradition can lead others to abandon new ideas in favor of selling old ones.

Step 5: Evaluate the Answer Choices

(B) is a perfect match. Like Marsalis, the research firm is trying to create new products that are similar to traditional products. However, that has just led to people abandoning the new products in favor of seeking out the traditional products.

(A) does not match. Here, the unintended consequence is comparatively higher price increases. There's no focus on traditional styles or abandonment of new ideas.

(C) does not match. Here, the focus is on people finding synthetic products less attractive. There's nothing about Marsalis's situation that suggests people are less *attracted* to new music than to old music—the record companies are just focusing on marketing old music.

(D) does not match, and is a 180 at worst. If anything, Marsalis is facing competition from established companies focused on profiting from archived recordings, not some upstarts with their newfangled ideas.

(E) does not match. In this scenario, somebody tries to save one thing (endangered fish), and a new thing comes along to destroy it. Marsalis, on the other hand, is trying to use old ideas to create something new, but it's the old ideas that thrive and diminish the presence of new stuff.

5. (E) Detail

Step 2: Identify the Question Type
"According to the passage" indicates that the correct answer will be directly stated, making this a Detail question.

Step 3: Research the Relevant Text
The question asks what Marsalis encouraged young jazz musicians to do. This is not a major part of the global theme, so do a quick scan for Content Clues, e.g., *encouraged* or "young musicians." Those words should direct your attention to lines 37–39.

Step 4: Make a Prediction
In lines 37–39, it is directly stated that Marsalis encouraged young musicians to "pay attention to [jazz] music's traditions." The correct answer should say exactly that, if a bit paraphrased.

Step 5: Evaluate the Answer Choices

(E) is a perfect match.

(A) is a 180, at worst. Even though Marsalis encouraged paying attention to tradition, the author claims Marsalis himself reinvented traditional elements for innovative purposes (lines 41–44), so it would seem unlikely that Marsalis would encourage musicians to restrain that kind of impulse.

(B) is Out of Scope. While Marsalis himself composed music, there is no mention of him encouraging others to do so.

(C) is Out of Scope. There is no mention anywhere of playing with older musicians.

(D) is a Distortion. In the same sentence that indicates Marsalis's encouragement to young musicians, it is said he also seeks to *elevate* the public perception, not ignore it.

6. (A) Inference

Step 2: Identify the Question Type
The question asks for something with which the author is "most likely to agree," making this an Inference question.

Step 3: Research the Relevant Text
There are no Content Clues or line references, so the entire text is relevant.

Step 4: Make a Prediction
With no reference point to start, there are too many possible inferences to make a solid prediction. Stick to the major themes and go through the answers one at a time. Eliminate anything that goes against the main theme and use Content Clues in the choices to test what's necessary.

Step 5: Evaluate the Answer Choices
(A) is supported, even if weakly. The support for this claim comes from lines 51–53. There, the author raised contrasting opinions regarding Marsalis's traditional views. To critics, Marsalis's classicism was idolatry, i.e., seeing past musicians as idols to be worshiped and emulated. However, at least Marsalis was creating new music. For record companies, classicism was just "play the old stuff again." They rejected new music entirely, making them a little more rigid.

(B) is a Distortion. Marsalis encouraged new musicians to respect traditional views, but it's never suggested that Marsalis directly promoted those new musicians personally.

(C) is not supported. The author does mention that both critics and fellow musicians were displeased (lines 7–9), but never suggests one group was more vocal. In fact, the author only presents the views of critics (lines 27–36).

(D) is Out of Scope. The views of younger musicians are never addressed in the passage.

(E) is a Distortion. The release of fifteen CDs is mentioned in line 12, but there's no indication that this had any impact on critical perception.

7. (E) Detail

Step 2: Identify the Question Type
The correct answer will be a question that is directly answered by a detail in the passage.

Step 3: Research the Relevant Text
With no Content Clues or line references, the entire text is relevant.

Step 4: Make a Prediction
With no research clues, a prediction is not possible. Instead, go through the choices one at a time, only doing research when necessary to ensure the question in the correct choice is answered.

Step 5: Evaluate the Answer Choices
(E) is answered in lines 53–58. It's money, of course. What else would encourage record companies to do this?

(A) is not answered. Marsalis didn't *release* any music in that time, but it's not known whether or not he was *composing* any music.

(B) is Out of Scope. No description of Marsalis's fan base is given.

(C) is not answered in the passage. This may be tempting for anyone familiar with Marsalis, who did indeed release such CDs. However, the content of Marsalis's CDs are not described in this passage, and this is thus not correct.

(D) is not answered. It is only mentioned that Marsalis did not have a contract. It is never actually said why.

Passage 2: Inferential vs. Noninferential Thoughts

Step 1: Read the Passage Strategically
Sample Roadmap

line #	Keyword/phrase	¶ Margin notes
2	but	Common belief: know own thoughts; infer others'
4	while	
5	But	
6	challenged	Studies with children dispute
9	while nonetheless	
12	but	
13	argue	Psych: people infer own thoughts
15	every bit	
16	According to	
19	It follows	
20	wrong	
23	so tenaciously; illusory belief	Knowing thoughts is an illusion
25	suggest; analogous to	
28	not only; but	similar to expertise
31	whereas	
32	For instance	
35	so	
36	expert	Infer quickly; don't notice
37	fail	
38	failure; leads naturally to	
39	supposition	
42	claiming	
43	perilously close	Auth: potential dangerous claim
46	But; in fact	But, psych. avoid problem
47	do not	
48	suggest	
51	e.g.	
53	explains why	Inferences made internally
57	Thus; crucial	

Discussion

The passage opens up with what common sense *suggests*: Presumably, we just know our own thoughts with complete accuracy, and we merely guess other people's thoughts. However, as could be expected in an LSAT passage, this assumption is rejected. The author presents a study in which children can accurately describe certain events, but have trouble describing their own thoughts about those events. From this, "psychologists argue" (line 13) that our thoughts are not directly observable; we're merely inferring our own thoughts, too, and we can be wrong about them.

The second paragraph presents an explanation why we insist that we know our own thoughts infallibly. Psychologists explain it through an analogy involving expertise. When we gain expertise in a field, it *appears* to change our knowledge and perception. We thought we were making inferences before and now just see the truth. However, psychologists suggest we're still making inferences; we're just getting so fast at making them that we don't even realize it. It's important to note the persistent use of phrases such as "it appears" and "the supposition." It's constantly suggested that people just *believe* they're observing things directly and infallibly, but they're not—they're just making inferences. That's a major theme of this passage.

In the third paragraph, the author brings up a potentially dangerous implication: Psychologists are almost saying our inferences are solely based on our external behaviors. *But*, the author qualifies that they're not saying that. Instead, psychologists say our inferences are based on internal activity in the brain. This activity is what makes our inferences so reliable and seemingly infallible.

There's a lot of psychological jargon here, but stay focused on the overriding theme. The **Topic** is our thoughts, and the **Scope** is whether we directly observe our thoughts infallibly or not. The **Purpose** is to present the views of psychologists (note how almost all opinions in the passage are attributed to them). The **Main Idea** is that, contrary to what people assume, psychologists argue that we do not know our own thoughts directly; we simply infer them, and those inferences are not based solely on observations of our external behavior.

8. (B) Global

Step 2: Identify the Question Type
The question asks for the "main point of the passage," making this a Global question.

Step 3: Research the Relevant Text
No need to go back into the passage. Just consider the Main Idea as predicted after reading the passage.

Step 4: Make a Prediction
The main idea is that, according to psychologists, we do not directly observe our thoughts infallibly, as is commonly

assumed. Instead, we're actually just making inferences about our own thoughts.

Step 5: Evaluate the Answer Choices

(B) is a perfect match.

(A) is a Distortion and a 180. This misinterprets the information about expertise in the second paragraph. Expertise makes it *appear* that we are observing our thoughts directly and infallibly. However, the psychologists argue that this is still just an illusion. Nobody is said to directly observe their own thoughts—not even experts.

(C) is also a Distortion and a 180. First, the psychologists' claims are not said to be "in response" to the common belief. Moreover, this contradicts lines 52–54, which state that we *can* make quick and reliable inferences.

(D) is a Distortion. The experiment with children is just a starting point for the argument made in the passage, not a primary focus. And the psychologists never blame anything on the lack of expertise.

(E) is a 180. This is the claim that the author says psychologists are "perilously close" to making (lines 43–46). However, the author immediately rejects that and suggests psychologists are *not* making that claim.

9. (C) Logic Reasoning (Weaken)

Step 2: Identify the Question Type
The question asks for something that would "call into question" an argument, making this a Weaken question like those found in Logical Reasoning.

Step 3: Research the Relevant Text
The question provides the line references for the primary argument, but it helps to consider the full details of the experiment, as described in lines 6–10.

Step 4: Make a Prediction
The psychologists conclude that people infer their own thoughts based on evidence of a study involving children. In the study, the children have trouble describing their thoughts about certain events. The psychologists assume this trouble is due to the children inferring their thoughts, and nothing else. To weaken the argument, the correct answer should provide an alternate explanation for why children have trouble describing their thoughts.

Step 5: Evaluate the Answer Choices

(C) is correct. If the children are stumbling due to limited language skills, then their inability to describe their thoughts may have nothing to do with making inferences. They may be seeing their thoughts directly, but just having a hard time expressing themselves.

(A) is a 180. This suggests kids are just as capable as adults at identifying their thoughts. That would mean kids are just as valid a source of testing as adults would be, making the experiment and the psychologists' deductions seem appropriate.

(B) is a 180. This suggests children and adults can be equally accurate (or equally inaccurate), which means children could be just as valid a sample group as anyone.

(D) is Out of Scope. The children don't have to know the difference. What matters is what the psychologists observe during the experiment.

(E) is also Out of Scope. Even if the study was intended for other reasons, it's still acceptable for psychologists to draw conclusions about other concepts from that study.

10. (E) Inference

Step 2: Identify the Question Type
The question asks what the author is "most likely to believe" regarding a claim from the passage. That makes this an Inference question.

Step 3: Research the Relevant Text
The claim in question is at the beginning of the third paragraph, but be sure to consider the context of the paragraph as a whole.

Step 4: Make a Prediction
The claim in question is one the author says psychologists are "perilously close" to making. *But* (line 46), the author immediately states that psychologists are *not* actually making that claim. The correct answer will indicate the author's belief that the claim in question is, ultimately, not supported.

Step 5: Evaluate the Answer Choices

(E) is correct. The author does not believe there is support for that claim—even if psychologists are perilously close to making it.

(A) is Out of Scope. The author never suggests that it's impossible to study thinking processes.

(B) is a Distortion. The claim in question is one that psychologists come close to making, but don't actually make. If they don't actually make that claim, then they can't possible misunderstand it.

(C) is a Distortion. The prevailing view that experiments undermine is the common belief presented in lines 1–5. The claim in question is not a prevailing view. In fact, the author says psychologists don't even really believe it.

(D) is a 180. The author claims that psychologists don't actually believe this view. And by saying that psychologists come "perilously close" to claiming it, the author suggests it's a dangerous idea and not likely to be "basically sound."

11. (A) Logic Reasoning (Parallel Reasoning)

Step 2: Identify the Question Type
The question asks for a situation "most closely analogous" to one presented in the passage. That makes this a Logic Reasoning question, specifically one that mimics Parallel Reasoning.

Step 3: Research the Relevant Text
The explanation for people's failure to notice they're making inferences is described throughout the second paragraph, primarily in lines 27–41.

Step 4: Make a Prediction
The failure is directly described in lines 35–38: We make inferences so fast that we fail to notice we're making them. Based on the surrounding lines, this is because we appear to grasp relations through expertise and just assume we're seeing things directly instead. So, the correct answer will describe someone who has developed expertise and assumes (incorrectly) that everything is now being observed directly.

Step 5: Evaluate the Answer Choices

(A) provides a good example. In this case, the anthropologist has become so familiar with his culture that he takes it for granted and just assumes he sees the truth—and he's wrong!

(B) does not match. This places a limit on studying something due to a requirement, which has nothing to do with the illusion of direct observation.

(C) does not match. The failure people have in the passage has nothing to do with an inability to go from abstract ideas to concrete experiences.

(D) does not match. Conflict of interest does not match the idea of making bad assumptions based on experience.

(E) does not match. We fail to notice our inferences because we assume we're seeing things directly, not because we're "too busy" doing something else and have to pass along the work.

12. (D) Detail

Step 2: Identify the Question Type
"According to the passage" indicates that the correct answer will be directly stated, making this a Detail question.

Step 3: Research the Relevant Text
The question asks about the result of gaining greater expertise, which is described in lines 27–32.

Step 4: Make a Prediction
According to the passage, greater expertise appears to change "our knowledge of [an] area" and our "perception of entities in that area," and it appears we are able to "grasp these entities and their relations directly."

Step 5: Evaluate the Answer Choices

(D) matches the described change in our perception and the way we understand (i.e., grasp) the relations in a particular area.

(A) is Out of Scope. Nothing is mentioned about *expressing* judgment about issues.

(B) is Out of Scope. Nothing is mentioned about taking a detail-oriented approach.

(C) is a Distortion. We may fail to notice we're making inferences, but that doesn't mean we ignore errors. You can't ignore something if you don't even realize it's there.

(E) is a Faulty Use of Detail. This refers to the sensations and emotions brought up in line 51–52. However, it is not suggested that we *reduce* our reliance on these sensations and emotions. On the contrary, they make it possible to make inferences in the first place.

13. (C) Detail

Step 2: Identify the Question Type
The question asks for something directly mentioned according to views "cited in the passage," making this a Detail question.

Step 3: Research the Relevant Text
The "illusion of direct knowledge" refers back to lines 38–41 ("the supposition that . . . we are perceiving [things] directly").

Step 4: Make a Prediction
The last sentence of the second paragraph states that "[t]his failure leads naturally" to the illusion in question. That phrase refers back to the previous sentence (lines 35–38), where psychologists claim that we make inferences so fast that we fail to notice we're making then. So, the illusion of direct knowledge comes from that failure to notice we're making inferences.

Step 5: Evaluate the Answer Choices
(C) matches the stated source according to the psychologists.

(A) is Out of Scope. There is no discussion of getting feedback on the accuracy of our inferences.

(B) is a 180. It is frequently suggested that we do *not* have unmediated (i.e., direct) knowledge of our thoughts.

(D) is a 180. It is often suggested that we *believe* our inferences are infallible (i.e., absolutely accurate), but that's not actually the case.

(E) is a Distortion. We make incredibly fast inferences which may not be infallible, but there's no suggestion that those inferences are in any way clouded or uncertain. We're certain we're right, even if that's not actually the case.

14. (D) Inference

Step 2: Identify the Question Type
The question asks for something that can "most reasonably be inferred," making this an Inference question.

Step 3: Research the Relevant Text
The use of children for the experiments is discussed in the first paragraph.

Step 4: Make a Prediction
According to lines 10–13, children have the same thoughts as adults, which makes them equally valid subjects. The difference, though, is that children are "much less capable of identifying these thoughts." That must have been the reason the study used children instead of adults, suggesting there's a benefit to using subjects that have greater trouble recognizing their thoughts.

Step 5: Evaluate the Answer Choices
(D) matches the prediction that the advantage comes from the likelihood of making mistakes (i.e., being less capable of identifying their own thoughts).

(A) is Out of Scope. The study is not about creativity, it's about whether thoughts are recognized directly or by inference.

(B) is a 180. It's the children that are more likely to be inaccurate, not the adults.

(C) is a 180. It is frequently suggested in the passage that nobody is actually infallible. Everyone makes inferences about their own thoughts.

(E) is a Distortion. The study is not about the ability to infer the thoughts of *others*. It's about inferring one's *own* thoughts.

Passage 3: Dowsing

Step 1: Read the Passage Strategically
Sample Roadmap

line #	Keyword/phrase	¶ Margin notes
2		Dowsing defined
4	For example	Ex. finding water
7	claiming	
16	skeptical	Skeptics:
17	crudeness	
18	assert	1) Crude tools = actually use subsconsious
23	Further	
24	skeptics say; while a few	
25	considerable	
26	success	2) Inconsistent results
27	generally is notably inconsistent; Finally; skeptics	
28	note	
30	unlikely	3) Hand-picked locations
32	Proponents	
33	contend	Proponents:
34	should be	1) Many techniques
35	also note	2) Studies skewed
39	Proponents	
40	claim	3) Sense electromag.
43	also claim	4) More successful than others
47	corroborated	Study supports proponents
57	significantly more accurate	
58	even	

Discussion

The first paragraph is very introductory, starting off with a definition of the **Topic**: dowsing. This involves finding things underground using basic tools. The definition is followed by a detailed example that involves finding water with a tree branch.

The second paragraph offers some opinions, which help identify the **Scope** of the passage: How effective is dowsing? According to the skeptics in the second paragraph, not very much at all. Their criticisms boil down to: 1) The methods are crude, and the tools do nothing—it's all in the dowser's subconscious; 2) studies show inconsistent results; and 3) dowsers just happen to go where success is statistically more likely in the first place.

The third paragraph offers a defense from proponents of dowsing. In short: 1) There are various distinct techniques, so you can't just lump them all together and judge; 2) studies tend to use inappropriate subjects who merely claim to be experts but have no certification; 3) successful dowsers are sensitive to underground conditions; 4) dowsers are more successful than scientists who use fancy schmancy tools.

The last paragraph presents a study that supports the last two claims of the proponents. In the study, dowsers competed against geologists and hydrologists to find water in a particular area, and the dowsers were more successful—even finding an area with *no* water when asked to do so.

The **Purpose** of this Debate passage is mostly to present the views of both parties about the efficacy of dowsing. The author does offer support for the proponents in the last paragraph, which may suggest some tacit endorsement of dowsing. But the overall **Main Idea** is pretty neutral: Some people are skeptical, but there is support that dowsers can find things underground effectively.

15. (C) Logic Function

Step 2: Identify the Question Type
The question asks for the "primary purpose of the second paragraph." In other words, it's asking for the function of the paragraph within the context around it.

Step 3: Research the Relevant Text
There's no need to reread the actual text. Just use the Margin Notes to see how the second paragraph fits within the overall structure.

Step 4: Make a Prediction
The second paragraph consists of the skeptics' criticisms of dowsing, the concept described in the first paragraph. Those criticisms are countered by proponents in the third paragraph.

Step 5: Evaluate the Answer Choices

(C) is correct. The second paragraph contains the arguments against dowsing, and the third paragraph counters those complaints.

(A) is not accurate. The second paragraph is entirely about opinions, not just supplementary details.

(B) is not accurate. There is one consistent point of view in the second paragraph, and there's no synthesis of points of view in the last paragraph.

(D) is a Distortion. The paragraph offers opinions about the details in the first paragraph. However, the opinions presented in the second paragraph are very broad and hardly "explore[d] in detail." And there are no ramifications to speak of. It's just a discussion of how one group of people finds something to be ineffective.

(E) is a Distortion and Out of Scope. The second paragraph only discusses one side of the dispute (the skeptics), and the third paragraph discusses the other side. No resolution is to be found.

16. (A) Detail

Step 2: Identify the Question Type
"According to the passage" indicates that the correct answer will be a detail that is directly stated in the passage.

Step 3: Research the Relevant Text
The skeptics' point of view is outlined throughout the second paragraph.

Step 4: Make a Prediction
The skeptics have a lot of complaints. However, the contrast Keyword *while* in line 24 indicates a brief concession: "a few dowsers have demonstrated considerable and consistent success."

Step 5: Evaluate the Answer Choices

(A) matches the skeptics' acknowledgment word for word.

(B) is a Distortion. Some scientists are mentioned in the passage (e.g., geologists and hydrologists), but any criticism toward dowsing in the passage is made solely by the skeptics, not any scientists.

(C) is a Faulty Use of Detail. This is the complaint *proponents* make in the third paragraph (lines 34–39), but there is no acknowledgment of this by the skeptics.

(D) is also a Faulty Use of Detail. Skeptics do claim that dowsers may be working subconsciously (lines 18–22), but the specific concept of being sensitive to Earth's electromagnetic field is raised by the *proponents* (lines 39–42), not the skeptics.

(E) is also a Faulty Use of Detail. Separate evaluation is encouraged by the *proponents* (lines 32–34), not the skeptics.

17. (D) Logic Reasoning (Parallel Reasoning)

Step 2: Identify the Question Type

The correct answer will have reasoning "most analogous to" that of an argument in the passage. That makes this a Logic Reasoning question along the lines of Parallel Reasoning.

Step 3: Research the Relevant Text

The skeptics' arguments are presented in the second paragraph.

Step 4: Make a Prediction

Unfortunately, the question asks for something parallel to *an* argument made by the skeptics, and they make a few. It's impossible to know which one to choose. Have a quick idea of the three arguments: 1) Dowsers' tools are crude; they're just using their subconscious; 2) studies show inconsistency; 3) dowsers just go where they're more likely to succeed in the first place. The correct answer will show someone consistent with one of these arguments.

Step 5: Evaluate the Answer Choices

(D) is perfectly parallel to the last argument. As dowsers just happen to go where water is everywhere and say "look, I found water!," the people in this answer just happen to go where fish are everywhere and say "look, I found fish!"

(A) does not match. The skeptics never claim there are tools that are more accurate than what dowsers suggest.

(B) does not match. The skeptics never accuse dowsers of having little evidence to support their claims.

(C) does not match. The skeptics never suggest that dowsers claim their abilities are innate, nor do skeptics suggest that any success of dowsing is due to intense practice.

(E) does not match. This may seem somewhat similar to the first argument, in which dowsers claim their tools work but it's all in the subconscious. However, the skeptics argue that dowsers' subconscious determination is based on "clues derived from surface conditions," not just thoughts of things that didn't actually happen.

18. (B) Inference

Step 2: Identify the Question Type

The question asks for something with which the author is "most likely to agree," making this an Inference question.

Step 3: Research the Relevant Text

The question asks about the study in the final paragraph.

Step 4: Make a Prediction

At the beginning of the paragraph, the author claims that the study corroborates the "last two claims" of the proponents. Going back to the previous paragraph, those claims were that 1) dowsers can detect changes in the electromagnetic field; and 2) dowsers can be more successful than other scientists. The facts of the study are consistent with both points.

Step 5: Evaluate the Answer Choices

(B) is correct. The study doesn't prove that dowsers can detect such changes, but the possibility is certainly there.

(A) is Extreme. While the dowsers may have had more success, that doesn't mean the other scientists would be "of little service to *any* groundwater-locating effort."

(C) is Extreme. The study may corroborate some ideas, but that's hardly the same as *proving* dowsing is the "most dependable."

(D) is Extreme and a Distortion. The study does nothing to show what makes dowsers *most* successful. Further, it makes no sense to suggest that dowsers used any tools other than their own.

(E) is a 180. While focusing on one type of terrain might indicate the study isn't a conclusive rebuttal, it definitely does *help* to refute some of the skeptics' arguments.

19. (D) Detail

Step 2: Identify the Question Type

The correct answer will be a question that is answered directly by a Detail In the passage.

Step 3: Research the Relevant Text

With no Research Clues, the entire passage is relevant.

Step 4: Make a Prediction

A prediction cannot be made here. Instead, go through the answers one at a time and research when necessary to make sure there is a directly stated answer to the question provided.

Step 5: Evaluate the Answer Choices

(D) is answered in the first sentence. Dowsing is used to detect resources (e.g., water) *or objects*—which suggests physical items other than water.

(A) is not answered. No timeline is given in the passage.

(B) is not answered. The effect of rain is not brought up.

(C) is not answered. Forked sticks are brought up as one method for finding water, but there's no mention of whether this is the most common or how it compares statistically to other methods.

(E) is not answered. Skeptics only broadly refer to using surface clues (lines 21–22), but never mention any specific clues.

20. (E) Inference

Step 2: Identify the Question Type

The correct answer is something for which there is "support for inferring," making this an Inference question.

Step 3: Research the Relevant Text

There are no Research Clues, so the entire text is relevant.

Step 4: Make a Prediction

With no clues, there's no choice but to go through the answers, eliminate those that are clearly wrong, and test the remaining answers as necessary.

Step 5: Evaluate the Answer Choices

(E) is supported. According to proponents of dowsing, successful dowsers "are not well represented in the typical study" (lines 38–39). However, the study in the last paragraph was extensive and used teams of "the most successful dowsers." Combined, that suggests the last study is not your typical study involving a poor representative sample.

(A) is a Distortion. The study in the last paragraph was conducted around narrow, tilted fracture zones. And while dowsers did find a dry zone on request, that is not to say the entire region was arid. Nor does that suggest that such fracture zones are more common in arid regions than in other regions. The comparison is unsubstantiated.

(B) is Extreme and Out of Scope. The passage only discusses studies related to finding groundwater, not other resources. Further, there's nothing to suggest that *no* reliable studies have been performed.

(C) is not supported. There's no mention in the final study what tools were used or whether they would be any different from tools used in different zones.

(D) is a Distortion. It is merely said that dowsers *were* able to locate a dry zone. That doesn't mean that other scientists *couldn't*. Perhaps they also did, or perhaps they just weren't asked.

Passage 4: The Use of Independent Research by Judges

Step 1: Read the Passage Strategically
Sample Roadmap

line #	Keyword/phrase	¶ Margin notes
Passage A		
2	?	Why oppose ind. research?
3	One; objections; distorts	1) Distorts system
5	undermining	
6	Another fear	2) Judges may research poorly
10	While; some merit; do	Auth: ind. research can be good
11	not justify	
12	First	
14	ill-suited	1) Good for specialized knowledge
19	Because	
20	considerable influence	
21	erroneous; detract	
22	could help	helps avoid errors
24	Second	2) Trial structure prevents bad results
25	reducing	
26	outlandish	
27	rather than	Supplements; doesn't replace
28	so	
Passage B		
30	Regardless	
31	should resist	Auth: Appellate should not use ind. research
33	As a general rule	
34	Thus; lack	Appellate courts lack live testimony and cross-exam
35	critical	
36	:	
39	And	Benefit of cross-exam
45	However	
50	Thus	No live comment
53	in particular	Usurps trial court's function
54	come under criticism; potential unreliability	
56	ignores	Ignores function of appellate court
57	questionable	
59	criticism	
60	full force	
61	regardless	

Discussion

The author of passage A starts with a question: Why are some trial judges against conducting independent research? As with most questions in an LSAT passage, this one is answered and serves as a focal point for the whole passage. The rest of the paragraph describes some objections: 1) Independent research can skew results and undermine other important evidence; and 2) judges may not have the best research techniques.

The author recognizes the concerns, but offers two reasons over the next two paragraphs why independent research can be good. First, in cases requiring specialized knowledge, the evidence raised by both parties can lead to conflicts and future problems that independent research can help avoid. Second, trials have a structure that reduces the chances of judges' research producing crazy results and ensures such research is a supplement to other evidence, not a replacement.

The **Topic** of passage A is independent research, with the author focused on the **Scope** of its benefits. The author's **Purpose** is to support the use of independent research. The **Main Idea** is that there are circumstances in which judges doing independent research is acceptable.

The author of passage B sticks to the **Topic** of independent research, but shifts the **Scope** to its use specifically in appellate courts. The author immediately suggests that appellate courts should *not* conduct independent research. That suggests the **Purpose** of this passage will be to explain why it shouldn't be used.

The second and third paragraph offer evidence against using independent research in appellate courts. Appellate courts lack the *critical* components of live presentation and cross-examination found in trial courts. The second paragraph focuses on the value of cross-examination, while the third paragraph explains why live presentation is valuable and how raising new information in appellate courts would steal that function from a trial courts.

The last paragraph wraps up the **Main Idea** that independent research is inappropriate in appellate courts and goes against the function of an appellate court as a court of review.

The passages are definitely of different minds about independent research. However, it should be noted that the author of passage A sticks mainly to its benefits in *trial* courts, while the author of passage B is more concerned with its use specifically in *appellate* courts.

21. (C) Logic Reasoning (Principle)

Step 2: Identify the Question Type

The question directly asks for a principle underlying both passages, making it a Logic Reasoning question of the Principle variety.

Step 3: Research the Relevant Text

The question asks about the overall arguments in both passages, so the entire text is relevant.

Step 4: Make a Prediction

The author of passage A argues that independent research is beneficial because it helps avoid conflict and supplements what is provided by the structure of the trial court. The author of passage B argues against independent research because it takes away the function of trial courts and goes against the function of the appellate court. Both authors are intent on making sure that independent research helps supplement a court's structure and function, not go against that.

Step 5: Evaluate the Answer Choices

(C) is correct. As the first author claims, independent research "supplements, rather than replaces" (lines 27–28) evidence from opposing parties. And the second author claims using independent research is bad because appellate courts would "substitute its own questionable research results for evidence that should have been tested in the trial court" (lines 57–59). So, both authors want to ensure independent research does not supersede the elements of a trial.

(A) might fit well with the author of passage B, but the author of passage A never makes a comparison between trial courts and appellate courts, so such a principle would be irrelevant.

(B) is irrelevant to passage B, which involves doing research in appellate court, which would take place *after* a trial.

(D) is Out of Scope. While the concept of questioning witnesses is raised as a side note in passage B (line 43–45), it's not a main part of the argument and has no bearing on the argument in passage A.

(E) is a 180 for passage B. The author of passage B weighs in on the reliability of some outside resources in lines 53–54, and cites the lack of their reliability as a reason *against* appellate judges using outside research at all. Furthermore, passage A makes no mention of what "[b]oth trial and appellate judges" should do and also does not discuss where outside research should have to come from.

22. (A) Inference

Step 2: Identify the Question Type

The question asks for something that "can be inferred," making this an Inference question.

Step 3: Research the Relevant Text

The question asks about both passages, and what should be done if judges *do* conduct independent research. That's raised in passage A in the third paragraph (lines 24–29), and in passage B in the third paragraph (lines 47–54).

Step 4: Make a Prediction

According to the author of passage A, independent research is guided by the structure of a trial and should be supplementary, not a substitution. And the author of passage B says that the appellate courts bringing up new information would "usurp the trial court's fact-finding function," which suggests that passage B agrees that independent research should be restricted to where it belongs: the trial courts, if anywhere.

Step 5: Evaluate the Answer Choices

(A) fits both authors' belief that independent research should conform to the function of a trial court.

(B) is not supported. Both passages raise the possibility of unreliable sources, but passage A does not lay out limits on the sources of outside research. Passage B warns of the unreliability of internet sources, but does condone the use of "reliable sources" as an alternative either.

(C) is a 180. Both authors argue that it should *not* replace such evidence.

(D) mixes the two opinions. However, passage A does not address whether it should be used in appellate courts, and passage B never directly argues that it *should* be used in trial courts.

(E) is a Faulty Use of Detail. Only passage B mentions this, and only in context of using independent research in an appellate court.

23. (D) Inference

Step 2: Identify the Question Type
The question asks for a phrase that conveys a particular meaning. These kind of definition questions are a variation on Inference questions. The definition won't be directly stated, but it will be inferred from the context. In this case, the correct answer will be "most closely related" to another phrase, which means this question also shares some qualities with Parallel Reasoning questions from the Logical Reasoning section.

Step 3: Research the Relevant Text
Start by looking at the context of the quote from passage A. That refers to judges who are concerned with their ability to "conduct first-rate research." This potential for bad research is addressed in the last paragraph of passage B.

Step 4: Make a Prediction
In the last paragraph of passage B, the author refers to the potential for an appellate court substituting "its own questionable research results" (lines 56–59), a sentiment echoing the concern raised in passage A.

Step 5: Evaluate the Answer Choices

(D) matches the prediction.

(A) refers to experts and their knowledge beyond what is printed. This has nothing to do with judges and their concern about their poor research techniques.

(B) is about judges participating in questioning witnesses, which does not reflect the author of passage B's concern about judges doing research.

(C) makes reference to live responses to information, which is not the same as being worried about researching that information in the first place.

(E) refers to using outside material, but does not mimic the concern about researching such material in a less-than-stellar way.

24. (B) Inference

Step 2: Identify the Question Type
The question asks what the author of passage B would be "mostly likely to take issue with," making this an Inference question.

Step 3: Research the Relevant Text
The question starts with a reference to lines 39–43, in which the author of passage B claims that parties in a trial can perform cross-examination on new information to ensure it is credible and reliable. This goes contrary to ideas presented in passage A about how scientific evidence "ensures conflicting and partisan testimony."

Step 4: Make a Prediction
The author of passage B does not share the concerns that scientific information will be definitively problematic. The correct answer will address this disputed concept.

Step 5: Evaluate the Answer Choices

(B) is correct. According to the author of passage B, cross-examination helps make sure specialized knowledge can be handled and introduced without a problem.

(A) is not disputed by the author of passage B. The first line of passage B is "*Regardless* of what trial courts may do . . . ." The author of passage B merely wants independent research to be removed from appellate courts, not trial courts.

(C) is Out of Scope for passage B. The discussion of cross-examination only applies to the trials at hand, not to future trials.

(D) is a 180. The author of passage B would not dispute this. If anything, cross-examination would confirm that erroneous decisions can be exposed.

(E) is a 180. The author of passage B does not dispute the structure of a trial court and its ability to involve independent research. Passage B merely argues that it goes against the function of an appellate court.

25. (C) Inference

Step 2: Identify the Question Type
This is a variation of Inference question that asks for defining a term within the context of the passage. In this case, the

correct answer won't provide the actual definition, but will be another word that has the same definition in context, which also makes this similar to Parallel Reasoning questions from Logical Reasoning.

Step 3: Research the Relevant Text

Start by looking at the word *crucible* in context. The entire sentence says that new literature introduced at the appellate level "cannot be tested in the crucible of the adversarial system." This refers back to the previous paragraph, in which the author discusses the testing of new information through the critical process of cross-examination.

Step 4: Make a Prediction

The correct answer will likely be a word taken from the second paragraph of passage B that directly relates to the process of cross-examination.

Step 5: Evaluate the Answer Choices

(C) is a match. The *engine* in line 42 directly refers to the process of cross-examination.

(A) does not match. This refers to a desire to conduct research, not the process of cross-examination.

(B) does not match. Cross-examination is used to test credibility, but it's the practice of cross-examination that is important (i.e., the crucible), not the credibility of the evidence.

(D) does not match. The function in line 53 refers to the purpose of conducting the trial (fact-finding), not a specific process (cross-examination) that is used in that function.

(E) does not match. This refers to the source of information (e.g., magazine, journal), which has nothing to do with the process of cross-examination.

26. (B) Logic Reasoning (Parallel Reasoning)

Step 2: Identify the Question Type

The correct answer will be a pair of titles that indicate a relationship "most analogous" to that between the two passages. That makes this a Logic Reasoning question, similar to Parallel Reasoning.

Step 3: Research the Relevant Text

Because it refers to the relationship between both passages as a whole, the entire text is relevant.

Step 4: Make a Prediction

The major relationship between these two passages is that they take different perspectives on the use of independent research. One supports it, and one rejects it. However, they both make their judgments in different contexts. The first just says it can be beneficial, while the second merely rejects its usage in appellate courts. The correct answer should have a similar relationship: The first supporting something in some

contexts, and the second rejecting that idea in a particular context.

Step 5: Evaluate the Answer Choices

(B) is a match, with the first showing support for something (salt) in some cases, and the second saying don't do it in a particular context (people with high blood pressure).

(A) puts a negative spin on salt in both cases, which goes contrary to the positive take by the author of passage A.

(C) is Half-Right/Half-Wrong. The first title nicely mimics how the author of passage A defends independent research against the concern of judges. However, the second title talks about inconclusive research, which is not comparable to the discussion in passage B.

(D) is Out of Scope. Neither passage advocates independent research as a substitute for anything, and the author of passage B does not talk about anything coming under fire (i.e., being criticized by others).

(E) is Half-Right/Half-Wrong. The first title definitely matches the supportive stance of passage A. However, the lack of something in a sample population does not match concepts in passage B.

27. (D) Inference

Step 2: Identify the Question Type

The question asks about the "stances of" both authors, which refers to their attitudes on a topic. And the question asks how those stances can be "most accurately described." So, the stances aren't directly stated, but they are directly deduced from the language of the passages, making this an Inference question.

Step 3: Research the Relevant Text

Both passages are entirely about independent research, so all of the text is relevant. However, the question does ask directly about its use by trial judges, so stick to that context.

Step 4: Make a Prediction

Overall, the author of passage A is supportive of trial judges using independent research as a supplement, even though judges' "concerns have some merit." While there's some suggestion that the author of passage B is okay with independent research in trial courts, the primary focus of passage B is still on the use of such research in the appellate court, not the trial court. In fact, in the very first sentence, the author claims that the argument about appellate courts stands "[r]egardless of what trial courts may do," indicating that the author of passage B ultimately isn't concerned about its use in trial courts. The correct answer should indicate attitudes of support for the first author and relative ambivalence for the second.

Step 5: Evaluate the Answer Choices

(D) matches the attitudes perfectly.

(A) is a Distortion in that the author of passage A never comes across as resigned, and a 180, if anything, as passage B never seems to disapprove of independent research by trial judges.

(B) is inaccurate in suggesting that the author of passage A is ambivalent.

(C) is a 180 for the author of passage A, who is not skeptical. And the author of passage B does not seem to be harboring hostility toward independent research by trial judges.

(E) is Extreme for the author of passage A, who is certainly supportive but not quite forceful. And the author of passage B is opposed to independent research at the appellate level, but not necessarily at the trial level.

Section II: Logical Reasoning

Q#	Question Type	Correct	Difficulty
1	Paradox	D	Check your online resources.
2	Inference	B	Check your online resources.
3	Assumption (Sufficient)	D	Check your online resources.
4	Weaken	B	Check your online resources.
5	Assumption (Necessary)	E	Check your online resources.
6	Principle (Identify/Strengthen)	B	Check your online resources.
7	Inference	C	Check your online resources.
8	Flaw	D	Check your online resources.
9	Assumption (Sufficient)	C	Check your online resources.
10	Principle (Apply/Inference)	E	Check your online resources.
11	Assumption (Necessary)	B	Check your online resources.
12	Paradox	A	Check your online resources.
13	Strengthen	A	Check your online resources.
14	Main Point	C	Check your online resources.
15	Inference	D	Check your online resources.
16	Strengthen/Weaken (Evaluate the Argument)	A	Check your online resources.
17	Inference	D	Check your online resources.
18	Role of a Statement	A	Check your online resources.
19	Inference	C	Check your online resources.
20	Flaw	A	Check your online resources.
21	Principle (Parallel)	B	Check your online resources.
22	Weaken	D	Check your online resources.
23	Assumption (Necessary)	A	Check your online resources.
24	Parallel Flaw	C	Check your online resources.
25	Flaw	D	Check your online resources.
26	Point at Issue	E	Check your online resources.

1. (D) Paradox

Step 1: Identify the Question Type

The question asks for something that "most helps explain" a situation. That makes this a Paradox question.

Step 2: Untangle the Stimulus

With Paradox questions, look for a surprising contrast. In this case, a small animal called the dunnart is born with thin skin, which is unusual because most animals of its kind need thick skin for body warmth and water retention.

Step 3: Make a Prediction

The mystery is this: How does the dunnart survive with thin skin if animals of its kind normally need thick skin? The author gives a hint by stating that the skin does get thicker as the dunnart matures in its mother's pouch. So, there may be something about that pouch that helps provide the necessary benefits of thick skin (maintaining body temperature and reducing water loss) until the dunnart matures.

Step 4: Evaluate the Answer Choices

(D) is correct.

(A) is irrelevant. Even with a respiratory system, the dunnart still has thin skin that won't help maintain body temperature or reduce water loss.

(B) is an Irrelevant Comparison. Even if this is true, the thin skin won't help maintain that body temperature, nor does this address the retention of water.

(C) is an Irrelevant Comparison. The paradox is about newborns, not adults.

(E) does not help. This does not address what happens at night, when temperatures may cool drastically. Nor does it address other dunnarts that may not live in such a fortunate environment.

2. (B) Inference

Step 1: Identify the Question Type

The correct answer will fill in the blank at the end of the stimulus. That blank is preceded by the Keyword [*t*]*hus,* which indicates that the blank will be a conclusion supported by the previous text. Something supported by the information given is an inference.

Step 2: Untangle the Stimulus

The author discusses stand-up comedians who can hold an audience's attention for hours and make interesting points. This is accomplished by using humor. University professors want to achieve the same results.

Step 3: Make a Prediction

If professors want to achieve the same results, then it makes sense to conclude that they should use the same technique: humor.

Step 4: Evaluate the Answer Choices

(B) matches the prediction.

(A) is not supported. It is stated that professors *hope* to achieve the same results as stand-up comedians, which suggests they may not necessarily have the same skills.

(C) is Extreme. The author is suggesting that humor might be a valid technique, but there's no suggestion it's the *only* solution.

(D) is Extreme. Humor may make some long lectures interesting, but that doesn't mean there's *no* way it will avoid losing the audience's attention. Even with humor, there could be something else that makes the lecture unengaging.

(E) is Extreme. Some comedians might be able to address certain serious topics using humor, but the author doesn't necessarily suggest humor would be acceptable for *every* topic, including the most serious.

3. (D) Assumption (Sufficient)

Step 1: Identify the Question Type

The argument presented will be logically sound *if* the correct answer is assumed. So, the correct answer will be a sufficient assumption, i.e., an assumption that is good enough, when added to the evidence provided, to guarantee the conclusion.

Step 2: Untangle the Stimulus

The reviewer concludes ([*s*]*o*) that the advice in management books won't be very useful for most managers. The evidence is that most managers are not CEOs, and management books are written from a CEO perspective.

Step 3: Make a Prediction

This argument, like almost all Sufficient Assumption arguments, is hindered by Mismatched Concepts. The conclusion is about the usefulness of the books, while the evidence merely talks about perspective. The reviewer assumes those concepts are somehow connected. More specifically, the reviewer assumes that readers won't find books useful if those books are written from a different perspective than their own.

Step 4: Evaluate the Answer Choices

(D) is correct. This is saying a book needs to be written from the reader's perspective to be useful, i.e., if it's not written from that perspective, it won't be useful.

(A) is not good enough. Even if this were true, there's still no evidence to support whether or not such books are *useful.*

(B) is Out of Scope. It doesn't matter what readers *want* to be. The argument is based on their current perspectives, and this offers no support for whether or not the books will be useful.

(C) is irrelevant. Even if CEOs were once lower managers, their perspectives could have changed when they became CEO.

Regardless, this is still not enough to reach the conclusion about whether or not the books are *useful*.

(E) is irrelevant. It doesn't matter what managers *prefer* to read. This still offers no evidence to guarantee the conclusion about management books and whether or not they are, indeed, useful.

4. (B) Weaken

Step 1: Identify the Question Type
The question asks for something that "undermines the mayor's defense," which means it will weaken that argument.

Step 2: Untangle the Stimulus
The mayor is being accused of taking a bribe in the form of home improvements to his vacation home. The mayor argues it wasn't a bribe. His evidence is that he paid every bill for that project that was presented to him.

Step 3: Make a Prediction
The mayor is trying to suggest he paid for the project. However, he doesn't say he paid *all* the bills for that project. He just claims he paid all the bills *presented to him*. What about all of the bills that were *not* presented to the mayor? If the mayor let somebody else pay for those (say, for example, a city consultant who wants to finance a nice project for the mayor in return for continued support), then his defense falls apart.

Step 4: Evaluate the Answer Choices

(B) is correct, attacking the mayor's presumptive suggestion that he was actually paying for the whole project.

(A) is Out of Scope. The mayor is merely defending himself. Whether the consultant took bribes or not is irrelevant. Even so, this choice only states that authorities are investigating the situation, which means it's still possible there was no bribery on anyone's account.

(C) is irrelevant. It doesn't matter who did the work. For the question of bribery, all that matters is who *paid* for it.

(D) is irrelevant. The actual cost doesn't matter. If the mayor paid for it, it's not a bribe.

(E) is an Irrelevant Comparison. The consultant's salary from the city could just be a legitimately sizable amount, and it doesn't matter how that salary compares to the cost of the mayor's vacation home improvements. All that matters is who paid for the mayor's improvements, and this offers no reason to question the mayor's claims.

5. (E) Assumption (Necessary)

Step 1: Identify the Question Type
The question directly asks for an assumption, and one that is "required by the argument," making this a Necessary Assumption question.

Step 2: Untangle the Stimulus
The archaeologist is rejecting a common belief, essentially arguing that humans did not need fire to migrate to the cold climate of Europe. The evidence is that the earliest controlled fires date back just 400,000 years.

Step 3: Make a Prediction
To argue that fire wasn't necessary, the archaeologist must believe that humans were able to survive in cold Europe before they could control fire. If controlled fire goes back 400,000 years, then the archaeologist must assume that people were in Europe before that time, and hence were able to survive without fire.

Step 4: Evaluate the Answer Choices

(E) must be assumed. Using the Denial Test, if *nobody* was in Europe earlier than 400,000 years ago, then the migration to Europe happened *after* fire was controlled. In that case, the archaeologist has no reason to suggest fire wasn't needed. So, the archaeologist must believe there *were* people in Europe earlier, before fire was controlled.

(A) is not necessary. The archaeologist's argument could be valid whether early humans used fire for cooking or not.

(B) is an Irrelevant Comparison. It doesn't matter whether it's colder now or it was colder back then. Was fire needed or not? That's the focus of the argument.

(C) is Out of Scope. Whether humans utilized natural fires or not, the argument is about the need for mastery of fire. This suggests people did use fire before it was controlled, but the archaeologist does not need that to be true to claim that *mastery* of fire was necessary for migration.

(D) is Extreme. This suggests that the need for heat was the *only* reason humans mastered fire. Even if that weren't true (i.e., even if humans would have mastered fire for other reasons), the archaeologist's argument is not affected.

6. (B) Principle (Identify/Strengthen)

Step 1: Identify the Question Type
The question directly asks for a principle, which will be found in the correct answer, making this an Identify the Principle question. Further, the correct answer will "help to justify" the argument, which means this question will also utilize the skills of a Strengthen question.

Step 2: Untangle the Stimulus
The astronomer uses a common argumentative technique: negating the views of an opponent. Some people argue that a space telescope project should be cancelled for being over budget. The astronomer says otherwise, i.e., don't cancel the project. The evidence is that cancelling the project would be a waste of the money already spent, which is greater than the amount needed to finish the project.

Step 3: Make a Prediction

The astronomer's argument is based on a principle of money. The argument would be justified if the astronomer held the same financial principle for any project: don't cancel it if the money already spent is greater than the remaining cost.

Step 4: Evaluate the Answer Choices

(B) is correct. If the space agency has already spent more than the remaining costs and is already over budget, then it has already spent most (i.e., more than half) of the total cost. By this principle, the project should be completed, i.e., not cancelled, as the astronomer argues.

(A) is Out of Scope. The astronomer does not refer to the agency's overall budget, nor how small or large the telescope project is with respect to the overall budget.

(C) is Out of Scope, and a potential 180. The project is said to be "way over budget," but there's no indication whether this means more than twice the original budget. In any event, this principle offers a reason to cancel the project, which the astronomer is trying to avoid.

(D) is a 180. This is suggesting that the agency shouldn't spend any more money on the project, which sounds a lot like saying the project should be cancelled—contrary to the astronomer's plea.

(E) is Out of Scope. The argument is not based on the likelihood of important new discoveries. Also, it's about whether a project should be canceled or not, not what should get funding in the first place.

7. (C) Inference

Step 1: Identify the Question Type

The correct answer will be "strongly supported by" the information provided, making this an Inference question.

Step 2: Untangle the Stimulus

The naturalist claims that different primates can behave in different ways. This is illustrated by two examples describing how two different primates (a chimpanzee and an orangutan) would behave if a zookeeper dropped a screwdriver nearby. The chimp would play around with it a little, then move on to something else. The orangutan would pretend to ignore it, then use it to tear apart the cage when the zookeeper leaves.

Step 3: Make a Prediction

Two very different behaviors, indeed. The chimp would act curious, but quickly get bored. The orangutan, on the other hand, would be quite cunning—playing it cool and waiting for the zookeeper to leave before carrying out the devious plan. The correct answer will be based directly on these observations. Don't make any assumptions about what this behavior *might* indicate. The correct answer must be directly supported. It's also important to note that these are just two

examples. Be wary of answers that make overly broad claims from these examples.

Step 4: Evaluate the Answer Choices

(C) is supported, as the orangutan is said to "pretend to ignore" the screwdriver, just to deceive the zookeeper into thinking nothing is going to happen—until the zookeeper leaves. Then, we've all seen Planet of the Apes, so we know what happens next.

(A) is Extreme and Out of Scope. Some might consider the orangutan's plan a sign of high intelligence, but that's not directly supported. In any event, the stimulus only mentions two primates. Without knowing how other primates would behave, there's no support that orangutans would be the *most* intelligent.

(B) is not supported. Walking away from the screwdriver doesn't mean the chimp has an inferior memory.

(D) is not supported. While the orangutan's plan might certainly indicate a dislike for being caged, there's no evidence that the chimp is any less displeased. Perhaps the chimp just didn't take the time to concoct as destructive and devious a scheme as the orangutan.

(E) is not supported. Walking away from the screwdriver does not necessarily indicate that the chimp didn't understand its use. Perhaps the chimp understood but just wasn't interested.

8. (D) Flaw

Step 1: Identify the Question Type

The question directly asks why "the manager's argument is flawed," making this a Flaw question.

Step 2: Untangle the Stimulus

The manager concludes ([*t*]*hus*) that Liang should not receive a bonus. The evidence is that bonuses only go to exceptionally productive employees, and Liang works in a division that is not exceptionally productive.

Step 3: Make a Prediction

Poor Liang; the manager is denying her a bonus because of the performance of her division. However, the rule for bonuses is based on the productivity of the employee individually, not the division that employee belongs to. The manager's reasoning is thus unsound, judging Liang on her group's performance rather than her own individual performance.

Step 4: Evaluate the Answer Choices

(D) points out the manager's error, judging an individual member (Liang) based the performance of her group (the whole division).

(A) is an Irrelevant Comparison. It doesn't matter how the standards compare from one division to the next. If the group didn't reach its own unique productivity goals, then the manager has a right to say it's not exceptionally productive.

(B) is Out of Scope. The profitability of the company has nothing to do with the argument at hand, which focuses on bonuses and productivity.

(C) is a Distortion. The manager uses a group's performance as a basis for judging one individual within that group, not for judging a different group.

(E) is Out of Scope. The manager is not assuming Liang won't be exceptionally productive in the future. She just wasn't productive this year (allegedly), and that's all that matters for the assignment of bonuses.

9. (C) Assumption (Sufficient)

Step 1: Identify the Question Type
The question directly asks for something assumed, and the argument will be logical *if* that assumption is in place, making this a Sufficient Assumption question.

Step 2: Untangle the Stimulus
The author concludes ([*t*]*hus*) that the journalist in question is definitely going to reveal her informant's identity. The evidence includes some Formal Logic: If the journalist's editor or a judge orders her to reveal the identity, she will.

Step 3: Make a Prediction
By the Formal Logic, there are two things that would ensure the source being revealed: the judge ordering it or the editor ordering it. The correct answer should confirm one of those two things will happen. There are two other ideas to consider: 1) The author states that the information concerns safety violations. It's unclear how this factors in to the argument, so it appears to be a glaring Mismatched Concept. There's a good chance the correct answer will show how concerns over safety violations will lead to a definite reveal of the source; 2) At the beginning, the journalist promised her source that she wouldn't reveal the source's identify—as long as the information is not false.

If	~ false	→	~ reveal
If	reveal	→	false

However, that doesn't mean the journalist will definitely reveal the source if the information *is* false, so that could be a trap answer. And even if the information is accurate, the Formal Logic suggests that a court order or an editor's order would supersede that and require her to break that promise. In short, the promise is ultimately a non-issue and should not be factored into the assumption.

Step 4: Evaluate the Answer Choices

(C) is correct. The information does concern safety. So, according to this logic, a judge will order the identity to be revealed. Thus, by the Formal Logic in the evidence, the conclusion is confirmed: the source's identity will be revealed.

(A) is not good enough. The journalist promised to keep the identity secret if the information was not false. However, that doesn't mean she would definitely reveal the identify if the information *was* false. That's an improper use of Formal Logic.

(B) is a Distortion. By this logic, it would be *necessary* that the information be safety-related for the editor to demand a name. However, it's not sufficient. Even though the the information is, in fact, safety-related, this logic does not guarantee that the editor will demand the identity be revealed.

(D) is a Distortion. Even if revealing the source is the only way to verify the information, that doesn't guarantee the journalist will break her promise and reveal the identity.

(E) is Out of Scope. What the informant understands is irrelevant. This shows that the informant wasn't ignorant. The informant knew that a judge's order would override any promise made by the journalist. However, it's still not said whether such an order was made, so there's no reason to believe the journalist would break her promise just yet.

10. (E) Principle (Apply/Inference)

Step 1: Identify the Question Type
The stimulus will contain a principle that will be used to support the correct answer. Because the principle is provided in a stimulus, this is an Apply the Principle question. And the correct answer will be directly supported by that principle, making this similar to an Inference question.

Step 2: Untangle the Stimulus
The principle is just one big piece of Formal Logic: If it's not difficult to return a borrowed item on time and the item's owner didn't say you could return it late, then you should return the item when you promised.

If	~ difficult AND ~ permission	→	return it on time
If	~ return it on time	→	difficult OR permission

Step 3: Make a Prediction
The rule is pretty straightforward. There are two things to note: 1) This rule only applies to people who promised to return it by a certain time, thus if no promise is made, then the principle doesn't apply; and 2) do not simply negate the

logic. If it's *not* difficult to return it and you *don't* have permission to keep the item late, then return the item on time. That's the rule. If it *is* difficult or you *do* have permission, the principle doesn't apply. It might be okay to return the item late, but you can't logically conclude that it absolutely is. Perhaps it's still the right thing to stick to your promise and get it back on time.

Step 4: Evaluate the Answer Choices

(E) fits the principle. A promise was made, returning the item on time is not difficult, and there's no permission to keep it late. Thus, as the Formal Logic dictates, the item should be returned on time.

(A) does not match. Even though Christopher gave permission to return the book late, that doesn't mean there's anything wrong with returning it early. The principle doesn't deny that.

(B) does not match. The Formal Logic contains the word *and*: If you don't have permission *and* it isn't difficult to return the item, then return it on time. Only one condition is met here (Wanda didn't give permission). If it is difficult to return the bicycle on time, then it may still be okay for Nick to return it late.

(C) does not match. Only one condition is met here: It's not difficult to return the car. However, Ted gave permission to return the car late, so the principle no longer applies.

(D) does not match. Yesenia did not promise to return the computer by a certain date, and the principle only applies to people who *do* make such a promise. While it seems reasonable to suggest Yesenia should return the computer on time, it does not conform to the confines of the principle in question.

11. (B) Assumption (Necessary)

Step 1: Identify the Question Type

The question directly asks for an assumption, and one that the argument *requires*, making this a Necessary Assumption question.

Step 2: Untangle the Stimulus

The author presents evidence of two gaseous substances. They both attract mosquitoes, but a bare arm attracts mosquitoes more than either one. The author concludes ([*t*]*herefore*) that the human arm must give off a different gaseous substance.

Step 3: Make a Prediction

This is a classic case of Overlooked Possibilities. The author has ruled out two possible gaseous substances and then concludes that it must be another gaseous substance. Why does it have to be a gaseous substance at all? Why can't there be some other aspect of the human arm that is attracting mosquitoes? The author does not consider that and assumes there are no other factors. The correct answer will state that

generally or introduce a specific alternative that the author assumes is non-existent.

Step 4: Evaluate the Answer Choices

(B) must be assumed. The author assumes the mosquitoes are attracted by a gaseous substance and nothing else—not even body heat. Using the Denial Test, if mosquitoes *were* attracted by body heat, then the author's persistence with gaseous substances would be seriously questioned.

(A) is not necessary. It doesn't matter whether mosquitoes communicate with each other or not. The argument is about what attracts them to the human arm in the first place.

(C) is an Irrelevant Comparison. The author does claim that mosquitoes are attracted to a bare arm "even in complete darkness," but that still could mean they're equally attracted in broad daylight. When the arm gives off more substances has no effect on the author's claims.

(D) is an Irrelevant Comparison. The argument is about what attracts the mosquitoes, not when they're most successful.

(E) is Extreme and Out of Scope. The argument is about what attracts mosquitoes. Whether or not our skin could ever repel mosquitoes has nothing to do with what happens when mosquitoes are attracted.

12. (A) Paradox

Step 1: Identify the Question Type

The question asks for something that would "resolve the apparent discrepancy" described, making this a Paradox question.

Step 2: Untangle the Stimulus

Two analyses were done on an Italian painting, one in 1955 and another in 2009. Both analyses found cobalt in the paint, a pigment not used until 1804. Based on that, the 1955 analysis logically concluded the painting was produced after 1804, *but* the 2009 analysis said otherwise—it was produced *before* 1804.

Step 3: Make a Prediction

If cobalt wasn't used until 1804, why would the 2009 analysis suggest the painting was *older* than that? The author must have omitted something critical about that 2009 analysis. It may be difficult to predict an exact explanation, but know that the correct answer will provide a reason why the 2009 analysis dated the painting to some time earlier than cobalt was first used.

Step 4: Evaluate the Answer Choices

(A) offers an explanation. The 2009 analysis showed cobalt was only found in upper layers that were added to older, damaged layers. If that's true, then the top layer with cobalt would be from after 1804, but the original, older layers could be from any time before that.

(B) does not help. Even if the new technology is more sophisticated, it still found traces of cobalt, so there's no explanation why analysts though the painting was produced before the use of cobalt.

(C) is irrelevant. It doesn't matter how many samples were taken. Cobalt was found in both cases, so there's no explanation why analysts would suggest the painting was older than the first use of cobalt.

(D) is irrelevant. Regardless of what the experts think, the painting still had cobalt, which wasn't used until 1804. There's nothing about the paint analysis that suggests it should be any earlier than that. So, if there's artistic evidence that the painting is older than 1804, then the mystery about the cobalt still remains.

(E) is a 180. This says that the use of cobalt in Italy, the source of the painting, was rare in the first few years after 1804. That would make it more likely the painting was produced even *later* than is suggested, when cobalt use was perhaps more common.

13. (A) Strengthen

Step 1: Identify the Question Type
The question directly asks for information that "strengthens the argument," making this a Strengthen question.

Step 2: Untangle the Stimulus
To reduce the spread of influenza, a campaign was run for six months to encourage frequent hand-washing and avoiding public places when sick. In that six months, there were fewer incidences of influenza, leading the author to conclude the campaign was a success.

Step 3: Make a Prediction
This is a prime example of Correlation vs. Causation. Fewer people got the flu during the campaign, so the author argues the campaign *caused* the flu rate to drop. However, the author may have identified the wrong cause. Perhaps there was some other reason people weren't getting the flu. The author suggests otherwise, assuming that people were, indeed, just encouraged by the campaign to wash their hands more and stay away from the public when sick. The correct answer will confirm this, making it more likely that the campaign was responsible.

Step 4: Evaluate the Answer Choices

(A) is correct. This offers more reason to believe people were washing their hands more often and thus listening to the campaign messages.

(B) is a 180 at worst. It's not mentioned what could help prevent the common cold. If washing hands and staying home when sick could reduce the risk of getting a cold, then this

suggests people weren't doing that. In that case, flu rates were down for another reason, not because of the campaign.

(C) is a 180. This suggests the campaign may have been irrelevant. There just might have been fewer opportunities for people to be at large gatherings where the influenza virus could be easily shared.

(D) is another 180. This directly offers an alternative explanation for the reduction in flu incidences. The campaign may have been irrelevant if people were just watching the news.

(E) does not help. This suggests that people recognized the importance of reducing the incidence of the flu, but it still doesn't show that the campaign was the factor that finally made people take action.

14. (C) Main Point

Step 1: Identify the Question Type
The question asks for the "conclusion drawn in the argument," making this a Main Point question.

Step 2: Untangle the Stimulus
The first two sentences provide factual results from a study. From these results, the author concludes that meetings need to have a clear, less-than-30-minute time frame to be truly productive.

Step 3: Make a Prediction
The correct answer will be a paraphrase of the conclusion in the last sentence, defining the circumstances needed to achieve maximum productivity.

Step 4: Evaluate the Answer Choices

(C) matches the author's claim that a clear, below-30-minute time frame is needed for maximum productivity.

(A) is a Distortion. This confuses the logic of the conclusion, which claims that a meeting "needs to have" a clear, less-than-30-minute time frame. That makes it necessary, but not sufficient. In other words, having that time frame doesn't necessarily guarantee that any such meeting *will* be maximally productive.

(B) is a fact from the study, and the facts are merely evidence to support the conclusion, not the conclusion itself.

(D) is also a fact from the study, and facts are evidence to support the conclusion, not the conclusion itself.

(E) is part of the facts, i.e., the evidence. Those facts are used to support the conclusion.

15. (D) Inference

Step 1: Identify the Question Type
The stimulus contains a set of statements, and the correct answer will be "strongly supported by" those statements. That makes this an Inference question.

Step 2: Untangle the Stimulus

The nutritionist provides an interesting contrast. Most fad diets prescribe the same nutrients to everyone, but not everyone has the same dietary needs. The nutritionist then tosses out a random recommendation to eat your fruits and vegetables.

Step 3: Make a Prediction

The opening contrast suggests that fad diets won't be appropriate for everyone. As for the fruits and vegetables comment, don't read too much into it. It's just a recommendation, but there could still be plenty of other foods that are equally helpful. The correct answer will conform to this limited information. Just be wary of answers that go beyond what's mentioned or exaggerate the nutritionist's claims.

Step 4: Evaluate the Answer Choices

(D) is supported. If different people have very different dietary needs, then those fad diets that tell everyone to eat the same few nutrients are not going to satisfy everyone's needs; hence, *some* people will not get what they need.

(A) is a Distortion. The recommendation to eat fruits and vegetables has no logical connection to the fad diets, so there's no way to conclude whether those diets include fruits and vegetables or not.

(B) is Extreme. The nutritionist recommends fruits and vegetables, but never goes so far as to say they are the *only* foods to provide widespread health benefits. There could be other such foods.

(C) is also Extreme. Not everybody has the same dietary needs, but that doesn't mean *every* single person is entirely different. There could be a group of people who all have one set of needs, but those needs are completely different from those of another group of people, whose needs are different from another group's, etc.

(E) is Out of Scope. There is no information about what foods contain what kinds of nutrients, nor is there information about which nutrients can be found in any given food.

16. (A) Strengthen/Weaken (Evaluate the Argument)

Step 1: Identify the Question Type

The correct answer here will help in "evaluating the argument," which makes this an Evaluate the Argument variation of a Strengthen/Weaken question. The correct answer will test the validity of the argument by questioning the author's assumption.

Step 2: Untangle the Stimulus

The caffeine in coffee can produce irritating stomach acid, but darker roasts (i.e., coffee produced by roasting the beans longer) have more NMP than lighter roasts, and NMP is something that helps reduce stomach acid production. (Don't

worry about what NMP actually is—all that matters for this argument is what it *does*.) *Therefore*, the author concludes that darker roasts are less irritating.

Step 3: Make a Prediction

It's good to know that darker roasts contain something that helps reduce acid production. However, the author assumes there's nothing else different about darker roasts that could counteract that benefit. Perhaps there is something else about darker roasts that could actually stimulate *more* acid production, despite the added NMP. The correct answer will question whether the NMP is enough to reduce acid levels overall or whether there's some overlooked factor.

Step 4: Evaluate the Answer Choices

(A) is correct. If the longer brewing time does increase the caffeine, then that could easily balance out the NMP, making darker roasts equally irritable. However, if the caffeine level is the same, then it is likely that darker roasts are better for your stomach.

(B) is a great question to ponder, but not relevant to the argument. The author merely claims the darker roasts will be less irritating by reducing acid production. Whether or not this causes other stomach function problems is an entirely different concern and does nothing to question the author's claims.

(C) is Out of Scope. There is no mention of coffees that contain less caffeine, and the author's argument is about reducing acid production, not reducing caffeine intake.

(D) is clever, but does not affect the author's argument. The author may well agree that more coffee (and thereby caffeine) could be consumed if the switch to dark roast was made, and if it was *too* much if might offset the benefits of dark roast. However, the conclusion was merely about the effect of darker roasts versus lighter roasts. Any change in habits beyond that are irrelevant.

(E) is Out of Scope. The argument is entirely focused on acid production. Other health benefits are interesting, but not relevant to this argument.

17. (D) Inference

Step 1: Identify the Question Type

The correct answer will be "strongly supported by the statements" provided, making this an Inference question.

Step 2: Untangle the Stimulus

The author mentions how difficult it is for film historians to determine how typical audience members respond to certain films. Two possible sources of information are presented as unhelpful: box office figures—which can't provide details about what people actually liked about a film—and movie reviews.

Step 3: Make a Prediction

In saying that box office figures "help little" and newspaper and magazine reviews "fail to provide much insight," the author is referring to how unhelpful they are in trying to determine the typical response from audience members. There's no indication what *would* be helpful, or if it's even possible. The correct answer should merely be consistent in describing the difficulty historians face, without bringing in outside information or exaggerating the claims.

Step 4: Evaluate the Answer Choices

(D) is supported. The last sentence says such reviews "fail to provide much insight," and that insight refers to historian's attempt to determine the typical audience member's view.

(A) is Out of Scope. The author makes no mention why historians don't find such reviews insightful, and there's no suggestion whether the reviews were generally written before or after a film's release.

(B) is a Distortion. The author mentions that it's especially difficult to determine audience views for early 20th-century films, but that doesn't make it *easy* to determine audience views of late 20th-century films. They may still be difficult to determine, just a little less so.

(C) is a Distortion. This confuses the detail that box office figures do not indicate what people find funny, frightening, or moving. However, that just means the figures won't reveal the specific components that people enjoyed. It's still possible those components are critical to a movie's success, even if they can't be identified directly.

(E) is not supported. The historians don't happen to find such reviews insightful, but that doesn't mean they weren't commonly written.

18. (A) Role of a Statement

Step 1: Identify the Question Type

The question stem provides a claim from the stimulus and asks for its "role in the argument," making this a Role of a Statement question.

Step 2: Untangle the Stimulus

The claim in question (the core would have a positive charge) is in the first half of the last sentence. Before dealing with that, consider the author's overall argument. In general, astronomers believe pulsars are giant balls of neutrons. (Don't get too caught up in the science. Simplifying the details into "giant balls of neutrons" is enough to stay focused on the structure of the argument.) At the contrast Keyword [*h*]*owever*, the author argues that this description also works for pulsars that are giant balls of quarks. As evidence, the author notes how a quark-filled pulsar would have a positive charge, which would attract particles that could "support a crust of neutrons"—thus

creating something that might be mistaken for the aforementioned "giant ball of neutrons."

Step 3: Make a Prediction

It's easy to get distracted by all of the science. However, boil the argument down to a simple structure. Scientists have a definition of something called a pulsar (it's a ball of neutrons). The author argues that definition applies even when it appears otherwise (when it's a ball of quarks instead). The author provides evidence that explains why the oddball pulsars still fit the original definition (a ball of quarks would have a neutron shell). The claim in question is in the last part, so its role is to provide evidence to show why quark-filled pulsars still can still have an outer coating of neutrons.

Step 4: Evaluate the Answer Choices

(A) is correct, identifying the claim as evidence to explain how non-neutron-filled pulsars (i.e., those filled with quarks) could still attract neutrons.

(B) is a Distortion and a 180. The author never challenges the idea that pulsars can be made of quarks. They absolutely can. And the claim in question explains how they work.

(C) is Out of Scope. The author says nothing about such pulsars going unrecognized by astronomers.

(D) is a 180. The claim actually shows how quark-filled pulsars *conform* to the consensus view, not challenge it.

(E) is a Distortion. The author never questions the mass of pulsars.

19. (C) Inference

Step 1: Identify the Question Type

The stimulus will contain a set of statements, and those statements will be used to "strongly support" the correct answer, making this an Inference question.

Step 2: Untangle the Stimulus

The analyst provides four requirements for the location of a particular generation station: 1) It needs to be near a natural-gas pipeline; 2) it needs to be near a large body of water; 3) it needs to be near transmission lines; and 4) residents won't oppose it. As of now, the analyst's country has extensive transmission lines, so the third requirement should be fine. The problem is there are only three large bodies of water near gas pipelines, but residents would oppose all three locations.

Step 3: Make a Prediction

With the residents being so stubborn (the author says they would oppose *any* construction project near the three bodies of water), the country is at an impasse. The only choice left is to find another body of water, but none of them are currently near natural-gas pipelines. That leaves one viable alternative if the country wants to build one of these stations: build new pipelines near another large body of water.

Step 4: Evaluate the Answer Choices

(C) is the supported inference from the analyst's information. The current sites don't meet the requirements, and building new pipelines is the only logical course of action if they want to build this type of station.

(A) is not supported. New pipelines can still be built, so there's no need to give up on natural-gas-powered generation just yet. Furthermore, perhaps existing natural-gas-powered generation stations would be sufficient to meet future electrical needs—it's only the construction of new ones that are cited as a potential problem.

(B) is not supported. The residents do oppose the currently available sites. If the station is built anyway, the residents might protest, but there's no indication they'd just pack up and move.

(D) is not supported. It's possible that such stations were already built in the past. The residents just won't approve of any *new* projects. The old stations could have been built before the public stated its views.

(E) is a 180. The analyst claims residents would oppose *any* significant construction project in those areas, not just electrical stations.

20. (A) Flaw

Step 1: Identify the Question Type
The question asks why the "reasoning is questionable" in the argument given, making this a Flaw question.

Step 2: Untangle the Stimulus
The author concludes that each generation of citizens is becoming more disinterested in politics than the next generation. The evidence is that people over 65 vote a lot while young adults don't.

Step 3: Make a Prediction
There are some representativeness issues with the author's argument; this is not an apples to apples comparison. What is true of a generation in the later stages of their lives may not have been true about them in their earlier years. Perhaps the younger generation will behave more like the older generation when they reach that point of their lives. Likewise, the older generation's current voting record may not be representative of their voting record when they were young adults.

Step 4: Evaluate the Answer Choices

(A) is correct. One generation is at an early stage of their lives and the other at a later stage. It is unknown how the older generation behaved when they were younger, and it is unknown how the younger generation will behave when they are older. So, the author makes a faulty prediction that the

young adults current behavior is indicative of what their future behavior will be.

(B) is not an issue. The argument is about percentages and rates, so actual numbers are not relevant.

(C) is accurate in that the author does not explain why people are becoming disconnected from politics. However, that's not the purpose of the argument, so there's nothing flawed (i.e., questionable) about omitting that.

(D) is Out of Scope. The author never addresses the cause of the problem, so there's nothing to confuse.

(E) is a 180. The point of the author's argument is that voting patterns *are* changing, and that future patterns are likely to show even more of a disconnect. However, the author fails to consider whether the older generation has always had a high percentage of voters, or whether they've matured into that behavior. If they've matured, then the current younger generation may do the same. Thus, the author overlooks the possibility that the voting patterns among age groups are *not* changing—it's just that older people may always be more likely to vote.

21. (B) Principle (Parallel)

Step 1: Identify the Question Type
According to the question, there is a principle to be identified from the argument given. However, the correct answer will not describe that principle. Instead, it will re-apply that principle to a new situation. That makes this a relatively uncommon Parallel Principle question.

Step 2: Untangle the Stimulus
The author concludes (*therefore*) that the city should not allow the office complex to be built just yet. The evidence is that building it would require draining a local marsh, and that raises potential problems that have yet to be assessed.

Step 3: Make a Prediction
In principle, the author is advocating not to take any rash actions when there are potential problems that should be studied first. The correct answer will apply this principle to another situation.

Step 4: Evaluate the Answer Choices

(B) matches the principle. Like the original argument, there are potential problems (recalls and lawsuits due to defects) that have not been studied yet. Based on that, it's recommended not to take action and sell the new product just yet.

(A) does not match. This outright rejects taking action because of the high cost of performing the needed assessment. That's not the same as temporarily holding back until the assessment is done.

(C) does not match. In this situation, the suggestion is to not reveal the results of the assessment just yet. That's not the same as asking the company to wait before selling the grills. In fact, it's possible the company has already started selling grills and sent some in for testing after the fact, which would go contrary to the original author's principle.

(D) is a Distortion. This tries to mimic the original argument's concern for the environment. However, the guiding principle of the original argument was not "do what's less damaging." It was all about assessing the problem before acting, and this argument leaves that out entirely.

(E) does not match. This simply makes a judgment that solving future problems overrides the costs involved. This does not compare to the original argument, which was based on assessing problems first. Further, this argument recommends taking a course of action while the original recommended temporarily holding off.

22. (D) Weaken

Step 1: Identify the Question Type
The question directly asks for something that "most weakens" the given argument, making this a Weaken question.

Step 2: Untangle the Stimulus
The author describes a study with two groups of people. The first group watched recordings of themselves on a treadmill. (That must have been exciting.) The second group watched recordings of *other* people on a treadmill. (Even more exciting.) When later asked how much they exercise, people in the first group reported an average of one hour longer. Based on that, the author concludes that watching yourself exercising can motivate you to exercise more.

Step 3: Make a Prediction
There is a lot wrong with this entire situation, but let's stick to the poor logic of the argument. First off, this is a classic case of Correlation vs. Causation. The author merely assumes that the videos motivated people, and nothing else. What's more, there's always a fundamental error when the author says something happened more often because people in a study *said* they did it more often. In this case, the people in the first group *said* they did more exercise. But did they really? Who knows? Maybe they just watched the video and thought, "Wow—I bet I exercise more than I thought. I'll just tell these research folks that I exercise a *lot*." If the correct answer doesn't show an alternative reason why people exercise more, it will likely show that people *aren't* actually exercising more; they're just making up numbers.

Step 4: Evaluate the Answer Choices

(D) weakens the argument, albeit in a very offbeat way. In the study described in this choice, people watched videos of their *identical* twin reading. In other words, they were watching people who looked *just like them*. After doing so, they overreported how much time they spent reading. So, they didn't actually read more, they just *said* they did. That

suggests the same might be happening with the treadmill study, and thus it is less likely that people are actually motivated to exercise more. Is that the best way to weaken this argument? Not by a long shot. However, it's the only choice that addresses either the assumption that there were no alternative causes of the increased exercise or the assumption that the people's self-assessments of more exercise were accurate.

(A) is an Irrelevant Comparison. The author is not concerned with finding the most effective motivator. If people exercised more after watching themselves on a treadmill, the author's argument is still valid, even if watching themselves lift weights would have been more effective.

(B) is Out of Scope. This involves hearing second-hand stories about other people. Even if that effectively motivates people, it doesn't weaken the idea that watching yourself exercise on video could also be motivating.

(C) is irrelevant. How many such participants were there? Did they make up a large portion of the study? And what group were they in? Without more details, a few stray health nuts are not going to have any effect on the author's claim.

(E) is a 180 at worst. This suggests that people *are* actually influenced by watching themselves on video. Watch yourself on a treadmill? You exercise more! Watch yourself sitting on a couch? (The most exciting video yet!) You sit around more!

23. (A) Assumption (Necessary)

Step 1: Identify the Question Type
The question asks for something the argument "requires assuming," making this a Necessary Assumption question.

Step 2: Untangle the Stimulus
The environmentalist is arguing that convincing people to reduce their personal use of fossil fuels is not going to reduce carbon usage overall. The evidence is that reducing carbon usage requires large-scale government policies.

Step 3: Make a Prediction
There's a major Overlooked Possibility here. The environmentalist is only looking at direct effects. Individual changes won't *directly* reduce carbon usage enough. However, it's possible that individual changes could *indirectly* lead to bigger changes, which may ultimately lead to the central requirement: government policies. The environmentalist assumes this wouldn't happen and that we need to start directly at government policies.

Step 4: Evaluate the Answer Choices

(A) must be assumed. After all, using the Denial Test, if personal changes *did* persuade people to get the government involved, then the environmentalist's argument is unsound. Focusing on individual efforts could pay off in the long run. The environmentalist must be assuming that won't happen.

(B) is Out of Scope. The difficulty in performing such calculations is irrelevant to the argument. The environmentalists's point is that people's efforts wouldn't be enough, even if they *did* go through the effort of determining the best course of action.

(C) is Extreme. The people encouraging personal reduction in fossil fuel usage don't *have* to be currently uninvolved in framing government policies. They could all be involved in government, but still fail, as the environmentalist suggests, by focusing on individuals instead of getting the government involved.

(D) is an Irrelevant Comparison. The argument does not depend on one course of action being easier. It depends on one being more effective.

(E) is Out of Scope. It doesn't matter which candidates people support. All that matters is whether or not the needed governmental policies can be enacted.

24. (C) Parallel Flaw

Step 1: Identify the Question Type
The correct answer will have an argument that is "similar to that" in the stimulus. Moreover, that reasoning is described as *questionable*, making this a Parallel Flaw question.

Step 2: Untangle the Stimulus
The author presents two possible sources of a painting's aesthetic value: the painting's formal qualities or its meaning. The author then argues that there's no valid support for saying it's in the formal qualities, so it must be in the painting's meaning.

Step 3: Make a Prediction
There may not be support for formal qualities, but who said there's any support for the painting's meaning? The author merely rejects one option without providing convincing evidence in favor of the second. The correct answer will follow the same flawed format: present two options, reject one for not having supportive evidence, and illogically claim the second option is correct.

Step 4: Evaluate the Answer Choices

(C) is a match. The author presents two options (economic or political forces), rejects one for not having supportive evidence (economic forces), and illogically claims the second option is correct.

(A) does not match. The author does reject one of two options. However, the original author claimed there were *only* two viable options. This author claims that there are multiple "other methods." So, this argument is flawed in that it fails to consider the other options, but that's not the same as the original argument. Furthermore, this author *does* give a viable reason to reject one of the two options specifically mentioned.

(B) does not match. The two options presented are requirements if an outcome occurs (the company being outbid). The author claims one option won't happen, so the outcome won't occur. However, this completely ignores the second requirement. And the original argument was not based on any necessary conditions. The Formal Logic is flawed, for sure. However, it's not the same flaw as the original.

(D) does not match. The author presents two outcomes if a situation occurs. The author then concludes that one outcome won't happen because the other won't happen. This displays some poor Formal Logic, for sure, but it's not the same as rejecting one option and saying the other option must be correct.

(E) does not match. If there are two options to consider here, it's whether the party changes its policies or not. However, the conclusion doesn't reject one and favor the other. It just says something bad will inevitably happen.

25. (D) Flaw

Step 1: Identify the Question Type
The question directly asks for a description of the argument's flaw.

Step 2: Untangle the Stimulus
The phrase "must be" indicates some Formal Logic. If there is to be economic growth, then there must be technological innovations. The author then claims that a ban on fossil fuels will spur technological innovations, and uses that to conclude that economic growth is imminent.

Step 3: Make a Prediction
When Formal Logic appears in a Flaw question, there's a good chance the author is going to commit the commonly tested flaw of Necessity vs. Sufficiency. Sure enough, the Formal Logic dictates that technological innovations *must* be in place first (i.e., they're necessary).

If	*substantial economic growth*	→	*tech innovations*

However, that doesn't mean tech innovations will guarantee (i.e., are sufficient for) economic growth, as the author asserts.

If	*tech innovations*	→	*substantial economic growth*

The author reversed, but failed to negate. The correct answer will describe this mistaken treatment of a necessary condition as if it were sufficient.

Step 4: Evaluate the Answer Choices

(D) is correct.

(A) describes the flaw of Circular Reasoning, but that doesn't happen here. The author misinterprets the evidence. It's not just about a mere restatement of the evidence.

(B) describes the flaw of *ad hominem*, which involves attacking people personally rather than addressing their claims. However, the author does not personally attack the critics of the ban. The author tries to addresses their claim, but fails to follow the rules of Formal Logic.

(C) is not even a flaw. This is suggesting that the author's evidence is *too* good. When's the last time you told someone, "I don't believe you—your evidence is just too convincing"?

(E) is a Distortion. This suggests the author concludes that innovation *always* brings about economic growth just because innovation *sometimes* happens before economic growth. That would be flawed logic, but it's not what the author does here. The author says substantial economic growth *must* be preceded by innovation, so, there's no *sometimes* about the author's evidence.

26. (E) Point at Issue

Step 1: Identify the Question Type

As with most Point at Issue questions, there are two speakers, and the correct answer will address something about which they both have an opinion. However, read the question carefully. Unlike most Point at Issue questions, the correct answer will be something the speakers *agree* with each other about.

Step 2: Untangle the Stimulus

Winston is unhappy with the rules for awarding Nobel Prizes. Each award can go to only three people, but many winning science results are the work of four or more people. Sanjay is also unhappy, but with another restriction: Winners have to be living. That ignores influential scientists who died before their results were recognized.

Step 3: Make a Prediction

Winston and Sanjay are both unhappy with the rules for awarding Nobel Prizes, particularly in science. In both arguments, the rules have the effect of denying credit to certain scientists (those who were left out after the first three people on a project were selected, and those who died before the project won the award). The correct answer will address this agreed-upon displeasure with people getting ignored.

Step 4: Evaluate the Answer Choices

(E) is correct. To Winston, the prizes are inaccurate because they only list three people and leave out other potential contributors. To Sanjay, the prizes are inaccurate because they don't recognize contributors who may have died.

(A) only addresses Sanjay's concerns. It's possible that Winston would agree, but there's nothing in his statements to directly suggest that.

(B) is a Distortion. It's likely that both authors want to see some changes to the science rules, but that doesn't mean science has to have its own unique rules. While both authors only talk about science here, they may have similar complaints about other disciplines as well. Perhaps they would both like to see universal changes so that the rules are consistent, but more inclusive, for all disciplines.

(C) is a Distortion. Neither author argues against the awarding of prizes to particular results. Their concerns are about the people being recognized.

(D) is Out of Scope. Neither author addresses whether the awards are based on subjective or objective criteria.

Section III: Logical Reasoning

Q#	Question Type	Correct	Difficulty
1	Point at Issue	E	Check your online resources.
2	Paradox	C	Check your online resources.
3	Main Point	A	Check your online resources.
4	Assumption (Necessary)	E	Check your online resources.
5	Inference	D	Check your online resources.
6	Paradox	E	Check your online resources.
7	Flaw	B	Check your online resources.
8	Main Point	B	Check your online resources.
9	Flaw	B	Check your online resources.
10	Inference	B	Check your online resources.
11	Parallel Flaw	A	Check your online resources.
12	Strengthen	A	Check your online resources.
13	Flaw	B	Check your online resources.
14	Inference	A	Check your online resources.
15	Flaw	A	Check your online resources.
16	Weaken	C	Check your online resources.
17	Role of a Statement	D	Check your online resources.
18	Assumption (Necessary)	D	Check your online resources.
19	Inference	C	Check your online resources.
20	Assumption (Sufficient)	E	Check your online resources.
21	Method of Argument	C	Check your online resources.
22	Weaken	D	Check your online resources.
23	Flaw	B	Check your online resources.
24	Inference	B	Check your online resources.
25	Parallel Reasoning	E	Check your online resources.

1. (E) Point at Issue

Step 1: Identify the Question Type
The question asks for something that two speakers "disagree over," making this a Point at Issue question.

Step 2: Untangle the Stimulus
Joe finds vampire stories absurd, arguing that these immortal creatures should have almost no prey remaining as they've been around for ages and all of their victims turn into vampires, too. Maria points out a flaw in Joe's analysis. In stories she's read, vampires only turn *some* other people into vampires, not *all* of their victims.

Step 3: Make a Prediction
The point at issue here is whether, in vampire stories, vampires turn everyone into vampires or just a select few.

Step 4: Evaluate the Answer Choices
(E) is correct. Joe claims this is correct, while Maria argues otherwise—in some stories, most victims are merely killed, not turned into more vampires.

(A) is Out of Scope for Maria. Joe mentions vampires' immortality, but Maria makes no mention of it, nor does she seem to dispute that claim.

(B) is Out of Scope for Maria. Joe mentions vampires existing since ancient times, but Maria neither addresses nor disputes that claim.

(C) is a Distortion of Joe's claims. Joe finds the stories absurd in that they have ridiculous consequences. However, that doesn't mean they're incoherent (i.e., confusing or unclear).

(D) is Out of Scope for both speakers. Joe argues that the premises of such stories imply that almost everyone should be a vampire by now. However, he never claims the stories actually depict this large-scale vampire population. And Maria never addresses how large the vampire population is said to be.

2. (C) Paradox

Step 1: Identify the Question Type
The correct answer will help "account for" the situation presented, making this a Paradox question.

Step 2: Untangle the Stimulus
A company wanted to help its salespeople by scanning all of their paperwork and storing it in a database that can be easily accessed by computer. They expected the salespeople would be thrilled. No more carrying around piles of papers! However, the result was not as expected. Salespeople resisted the database and refused to get their paperwork scanned.

Step 3: Make a Prediction
It definitely seems strange that the salespeople were not interested in something that seems so helpful. Why did they resist this change? The most likely explanations are that there

was something remarkably inconvenient about the database, or there is something highly beneficial about keeping work in paper form. The correct answer will address one, if not both, of these possible explanations.

Step 4: Evaluate the Answer Choices
(C) is correct. This points to a benefit of paper forms—client confidentiality. That explains why salespeople resisted the database and didn't want to submit their paperwork for scanning.

(A) does not help. This confirms that some salespeople didn't submit a lot of paperwork. However, it doesn't offer a reason why, so there's still no accounting for their resistance.

(B) is a 180. If the salespeople *didn't* have portable computers, that might explain why they resisted the database. However, if they already had portable computers, it's even more unusual that they wouldn't take advantage of the database.

(D) is a 180, at worst. If the training was inconvenient and the database was overly complicated, that might explain the resistance. However, if the salespeople found the database software so easy to use, it's even harder to understand why they wouldn't use it.

(E) is Out of Scope. The paradox has nothing to do with the building of the database. The paradox is all about why employees didn't *use* the database, no matter how much time or money it cost to build.

3. (A) Main Point

Step 1: Identify the Question Type
The question asks you what "the politician argues," which means the correct answer should express the point the politician is advocating, i.e., the main point.

Step 2: Untangle the Stimulus
The politician is making a common claim that "free speech" doesn't imply everything you say is protected. What follows are some common examples of unacceptable forms of speech, which all lead to the ultimate conclusion: Some forms of speech can lead directly to harm and are thus okay to make illegal.

Step 3: Make a Prediction
The correct answer will express the politician's claim at the end that criminalization of some speech is okay because that speech can cause harm.

Step 4: Evaluate the Answer Choices
(A) is correct.

(B) is Extreme. The politician uses examples of speech that can cause harm and concludes that such speech can be restricted. However, the author doesn't claim this is the *only* kind of speech that can be restricted. There may be other reasons to restrict other kinds of speech.

(C) is a Distortion. The only harm mentioned by the politician is that caused by certain forms of speech. The author never says anything about harm being caused by restricting speech.

(D) is Extreme. The politician argues that certain forms of speech can lead directly to harm, but never says that *any* form of speech can do so.

(E) is Out of Scope. The author never mentions any situation in which restricting freedom is *un*justified.

4. (E) Assumption (Necessary)

Step 1: Identify the Question Type
The question directly asks for an assumption on which the argument *depends*, making this a Necessary Assumption question.

Step 2: Untangle the Stimulus
According to the art critic, people who go to museums look at an artwork for under a minute, take a photo, and move on. That leads the critic to conclude that people are less willing to engage with artwork.

Step 3: Make a Prediction
This is a perfect example of Mismatched Concepts. The evidence is all about the brief time spent looking at artwork, but the conclusion raises the concept of being engaged. The art critic is assuming there's a connection between those two concepts, i.e., that time spent looking at an artwork somehow indicates how engaged one is with that artwork.

Step 4: Evaluate the Answer Choices

(E) is correct. By the Denial Test, if time spent was *not* a reliable measure of engagement, then the critic's conclusion is completely unsupported. The art critic must assume that time spent has some connection to engagement.

(A) is Out of Scope. It doesn't matter whether people see one piece of art or 100. The argument is about whether people are engaged with that art, and this makes no connection to that.

(B) is irrelevant. Why people move so quickly doesn't matter. What matters is whether or not people are losing their willingness to engage in the art.

(C) is Out of Scope. The argument is not about enjoying the museum-going experience. It's about engaging with the artwork, which is not necessarily the same concept.

(D) is Out of Scope. This may strengthen the art critic's evidence that people don't spend much time with a single piece of art—they don't even look at the photo of the art! However, regardless of the time spent with the artwork or its photo, this offers no connection to whether or not people feel engaged with the artwork.

5. (D) Inference

Step 1: Identify the Question Type
The correct answer will be "supported by the information" given, making this an Inference question.

Step 2: Untangle the Stimulus
According to the author, heavy tapestry fabrics shouldn't be used to create items that need to be frequently laundered, such as clothing. Instead, it should be used for items such as window treatments.

Step 3: Make a Prediction
The word *only* indicates Formal Logic: If it's appropriate to use heavy fabric, then the item should not be frequently laundered. By contrapositive, if an item is going to be frequently laundered, then it's not appropriate to use heavy tapestry fabrics.

If	heavy fabric appropriate	→	~ laundered frequently
If	laundered frequently	→	~ heavy fabric appropriate

The correct answer will follow this logic without improperly negating or reversing the logic.

Step 4: Evaluate the Answer Choices

(D) is correct, essentially using the contrapositive. Because skirts and jackets are said to be frequently laundered clothing, then heavy fabric would not be appropriate.

(A) is a Distortion. Heavy fabrics are appropriate for swags, but there could be other fabrics not mentioned that are also appropriate.

(B) is Extreme. The author says that appropriate applications *include* swags and balloon valances. However, there are likely plenty of other acceptable applications for heavy fabrics.

(C) is also Extreme. Appropriate applications *include* the window treatments listed, but that doesn't mean all appropriate applications *must* be window treatments.

(E) is a 180. The author specifically makes note of skirts and jackets, but the general claim is that heavy tapestry fabrics are not appropriate for "any types of clothing."

6. (E) Paradox

Step 1: Identify the Question Type
The question asks for something that "helps to explain" a discrepancy, making this a Paradox question.

Step 2: Untangle the Stimulus
New apartments in Brewsterville logically increased the supply of available housing. However, while that usually

leads to lower rents for existing apartments, the opposite happened: those rents went up.

Step 3: Make a Prediction
Why did rents for existing apartments go up when they usually go down? The correct answer will answer that question. The correct answer will likely show why even the existing apartments (instead of just the new ones) are suddenly more desirable.

Step 4: Evaluate the Answer Choices

(E) solves the mystery. If the population stayed the same, then the general trend would be expected: high prices for the new apartments and lower prices for the old ones. However, if lots of people are looking to move in to the area, then there would be increased demand for both the new *and* the existing apartments, which would logically lead to the higher prices.

(A) does not help. Even if there were supposed to be more new apartments, there's no indication why the older apartments are more desirable and worth more rent.

(B) is a 180. If the new apartments are more desirable, then they should have higher rents. It wouldn't make sense to raise the rent for the old apartments, which are less desirable.

(C) is Out of Scope. The effect in other areas has no impact on explaining the rent increase on apartments in Brewsterville.

(D) does not help. This just suggests that there were more older apartments available as people moved out. However, with more apartments available, that doesn't explain why the rent would increase.

7. (B) Flaw

Step 1: Identify the Question Type
The correct answer will describe why the argument is "vulnerable to criticism," a frequently used phrase that indicates a Flaw question.

Step 2: Untangle the Stimulus
The author argues that politicians push for more economic productivity but ignore the negative consequences. The author then provides an example of how a company could attempt to increase productivity by increasing profits, but that often leads to reducing employment. *Thus*, the author concludes that trying to increase economic productivity would lead to unemployment.

Step 3: Make a Prediction
The author provides a great example of how focusing on productivity can have undesirable consequences. However, the author then uses the details of that one example (about a corporation losing employees) and suggests the exact same consequences will happen if politicians focus on increasing economic productivity as a whole. While it's possible that focusing too much on productivity could be problematic,

there's no reason to suggest that the result would *definitely* be unemployment based on one hypothetical example. This is a common flaw of basing a broad conclusion on an unrepresentative sample.

Step 4: Evaluate the Answer Choices

(B) correctly describes the commonly tested flaw. The author assumes that what happens in one single case is going to happen when addressing the economy overall.

(A) is Out of Scope. The author is certainly concerned about potential drawbacks, particularly unemployment. However, the author never argues that the goal of increasing productivity should be *abandoned*. Perhaps the author just feels that politicians should exercise more caution.

(C) is a Distortion. The author does criticize politicians in general, but the evidence is that they do, in general, fail to consider the drawbacks. It's not said to be just a few politicians that make this mistake.

(D) is a Distortion. The author makes no comparison as to whose interests are more important. Besides, the author claims that increasing productivity would be beneficial to business owners, so there's no assumption that productivity is more important than the owners' interests.

(E) is a Distortion. The author's argument is just that there can be drawbacks, not that the drawbacks outweigh the benefits. To claim that there are drawbacks, the author merely needs to show they exist. There's no need to mention *all* drawbacks or any benefits.

8. (B) Main Point

Step 1: Identify the Question Type
The question asks for the "overall conclusion," i.e., the main point of the argument.

Step 2: Untangle the Stimulus
The author starts with the opinion that good movie reviewers should be able to give positive reviews to movies they don't personally like. This opinion is supported by two facts: 1) Movie reviewers' tastes are often very different from those of most moviegoers; and 2) the role of a movie reviewer is to help people decide which movies they might enjoy.

Step 3: Make a Prediction
In an argument, the conclusion is an opinion that is supported by evidence, which usually consists of facts. In this argument, the only true opinion is the first sentence, and that claim is supported by the facts provided. So, the conclusion is that good movie reviewers should be able to give positive reviews to movies they don't personally like.

Step 4: Evaluate the Answer Choices

(B) is correct, providing an accurate paraphrase of the conclusion in the first sentence.

(A) is a subsidiary conclusion presented in the argument as evidence to support the main conclusion; its not the main conclusion itself.

(C) is a fact presented in the argument, and facts are part of the evidence, not the conclusion.

(D) is a fact, that is used to support the subsidiary conclusion that movie reviewers have tastes that are typically different and better informed than most moviegoers.

(E) is a fact presented as evidence to support the conclusion, not the conclusion itself.

9. (B) Flaw

Step 1: Identify the Question Type
The question directly asks for the flaw in the argument.

Step 2: Untangle the Stimulus
The author presents a correlation: a certain part of the brain tends to be larger in skilled musicians than in people who don't really play music. This leads the author to conclude that playing an instrument changes the brain's structure.

Step 3: Make a Prediction
This is a prime example of the flaw of correlation vs. causation. The brain area happens to be larger in musicians (a correlation), so the author assumes that playing music is the *cause* of that area being larger. There are three problems with such causal arguments: 1) The author overlooks other causes, i.e., other factors that contribute to the size of the brain area; 2) the author may have reversed the causality, i.e., already having a larger brain area may be responsible for people choosing to play music, not the other way around; and 3) it's just a coincidence, i.e., the results are correlated but neither one directly affects the other. The correct answer will express one of these three problems.

Step 4: Evaluate the Answer Choices

(B) is correct, identifying the overlooked possibility that the author has the causality reversed, i.e., that having a larger brain area causes people to play music, not the other way around.

(A) is an Irrelevant Comparison. The author mentions piano sounds, but attributes the ability to all musicians equally. There is no comparison made or assumed about pianists versus other musicians.

(C) is a Out of Scope. The author indicates highly skilled musicians have a specific area of their brain that is larger. The author claims this is caused by playing an instrument. The author does not then take this supposed phenomenon and apply it broadly to other activities that could also (allegedly) change brain structure.

(D) is Out of Scope. The author is merely suggesting that playing an instrument can affect one particular area of the brain. That doesn't mean listening to music can't affect

another area. That has no bearing on the author's argument, so the author has no need to address it.

(E) is also Out of Scope. The argument is about how playing music affects a particular part of the brain. What makes someone a highly skilled musician or how much practice is involved is entirely irrelevant.

10. (B) Inference

Step 1: Identify the Question Type
The stimulus will provide a set of statements that will "strongly support" the correct answer, making this an Inference question.

Step 2: Untangle the Stimulus
According to the researcher, hearing just one side of a cell-phone conversation can be distracting for two reasons: 1) The listener starts to guess what the other side is saying; and 2) the cell-phone user speaks very loudly.

Step 3: Make a Prediction
There is very little to work with here, and thus very little to predict. The correct answer will be consistent with the distracting quality of hearing one side of a cell-phone conversation. Watch out for answers that exaggerate or distort these claims.

Step 4: Evaluate the Answer Choices

(B) is correct. According to the first claim, overhearing a cell-phone conversation can divert attention from *whatever* someone is doing. That would include an activity such as driving.

(A) is a Distortion. People are said to be distracted if they hear one side of a conversation, i.e., they hear somebody *else* on a cell-phone. If a driver is talking on the phone, the driver is hearing both sides, not just one. While, in real life, this statement is probably very true, it is not supported by the information provided.

(C) is a 180, at worst. The statements only support what happens when people hear one side of a call on a cell-phone, not a traditional phone. Besides, the first distraction (listeners guessing what the other side is saying) could still apply to traditional phones, which would likely make hearing one side of a traditional phone conversation similarly distracting.

(D) is Extreme. Overhearing one side of a cell-phone call might divert one's attention, but perhaps just temporarily. That doesn't necessarily mean people will completely lose track of their thoughts.

(E) is Out of Scope. The situation described is guessing what people are saying when you can't hear them, not guessing what people mean when you *do* hear them. This also makes an unsupported comparison between cell-phone conversations and other forms of conversations, which are never addressed.

11. (A) Parallel Flaw

Step 1: Identify the Question Type

The correct answer will use "parallel reasoning" to indicate the "flawed nature" of the argument provided, making this a Parallel Flaw question.

Step 2: Untangle the Stimulus

The author mentions that studies showed positive results for a promising new pain treatment. However, there was something wrong with the method for each study, so the author concludes the pain treatment is probably no good.

Step 3: Make a Prediction

The study methods may have been flawed in some way, but the results could still have been accurate. The author doesn't consider that, and the correct answer will describe a situation that commits the same flaw: Concluding that something assessed as good is likely bad because of some problem with how that item was assessed.

Step 4: Evaluate the Answer Choices

(A) is a match. The cake was assessed as good (it won the contest), but the author argues that it's probably bad because of some problem with how the cake was assessed (the criteria was not consistent). Even with inconsistent criteria, the cake could still be good, just as the pain treatment in the original argument could still be effective, despite the flawed methods in the studies.

(B) does not match. There is no judging the quality of anything or questioning the method of assessment.

(C) does not match. No method of assessment is addressed, and this author shifts from a discussion of nutritional value to a conclusion of being malnourished, a shift in scope that was never found in the original argument.

(D) does not match. No method of assessment is addressed, and the author does not claim that a positive judgment is likely wrong.

(E) does not match. This does not address any method of assessment, and the author does not say something claimed to be good is likely bad.

12. (A) Strengthen

Step 1: Identify the Question Type

The question asks for something that "strongly supports the argument" given, making this a Strengthen question.

Step 2: Untangle the Stimulus

The conclusion is a conditional prediction: If computer simulations can test safety features as effectively as test crashes, then companies will use fewer test crashes. The evidence is that computer simulations would cost a lot less.

Step 3: Make a Prediction

This is a case of Overlooked Possibilities. If test crashes are more expensive, that could certainly provide an incentive to cut back on using them. However, the author's prediction is based on computers being equally effective in providing information about safety features. What if test crashes are used to produce more than just safety information? The author doesn't consider that and assumes there are no other benefits to test crashes that would warrant keeping them around, even if computer simulations were to provide equally reliable safety information. The correct answer will validate this assumption.

Step 4: Evaluate the Answer Choices

(A) is correct, confirming that most of the important information gleaned from test crashes is, indeed, safety-related.

(B) is a Distortion. The author's prediction is based on the condition that computer simulations become more informative. However, even if that were likely, as this choice suggests, that doesn't help verify that the prediction is any more valid. The same assumptions and overlooked possibilities persist.

(C) is Out of Scope. The author's argument is not about creating safer cars. The author just seems more intent on finding a cheaper way to test them.

(D) is a 180. The cost of designing the features has no impact on the argument, as the argument is solely about testing the features. Nonetheless, if the cost of testing is decreasing and is predicted to decrease further, then it may eventually be just as cheap as computer simulations. In that case, there'd be no need to cut back on test crashes.

(E) is an Irrelevant Comparison. What the aviation industry needs is not necessarily comparable to what the automobile industry needs. For the auto industry, there could still be particular needs served by test crashes that would not be served by computer simulations.

13. (B) Flaw

Step 1: Identify the Question Type

The correct answer will describe how the argument is "vulnerable to criticism," common wording used to indicate a Flaw question.

Step 2: Untangle the Stimulus

The legislator concludes ([s]o) that a certain act should be approved. The evidence is that a colleague recommends rejecting the act because it would deter investment. However, the legislator questions that reasoning because the colleague favored other acts in the past that deterred investment.

Step 3: Make a Prediction

The legislator is making an *ad hominem* attack. The legislator is questioning the colleague merely on her previous actions. It's possible that the colleague *is* against deterring investment, but there was an overriding concern to the earlier legislation. Instead of attacking the colleague personally for her previous voting record, the legislator should have focused on her reasoning for rejecting this act. The correct answer will describe this flaw.

Step 4: Evaluate the Answer Choices

(B) is correct, describing the legislator's failure to address the colleague's reasoning, instead concentrating on her previous voting record.

(A) is a Distortion. Attacking one's character traits is a form of *ad hominem* attack, but the legislator is not doing that. The legislator is attacking the colleague's prior actions, not her character traits.

(C) is Out of Scope. The legislator does not address which position is more popular, and does not assume either way.

(D) is Out of Scope. The legislator does not assume anything about voters. This argument is solely about the colleague's opinion and the reason to be skeptical of that.

(E) is also Out of Scope. If anything, the legislator would welcome this information as it would show a reason why the colleague's reasoning is not persuasive. The colleague doesn't really care about investment; she's just trying to placate her constituents.

14. (A) Inference

Step 1: Identify the Question Type

The correct answer would logically fill in the blank at the end of the argument given. The blank is preceded by the conclusion Keyword *so*, indicating that the blank will contain a conclusion directly supported by the given evidence. That makes this an Inference question.

Step 2: Untangle the Stimulus

The first claim is Formal Logic: To increase efficiency significantly, a computer system needs to make employees adopt a new way of working.

	efficiency		adapt new
If	significantly	→	productive
	up		ways

Then, the author claims that the new computer system for the Ministry of Transportation will fit the way employees currently work.

Step 3: Make a Prediction

The new system for the Ministry of Transportation fails to meet the necessary condition for increasing efficiency. If it

merely fits with existing ways of working, then employees don't need to adopt a new way of working. The sufficient term of the contrapositive is triggered.

	~ adapt new		efficiency
If	productive ways	→	~ significantly
			up

Thus, by the Formal Logic in the first statement, the logical conclusion is that the new system will not increase efficiency.

Step 4: Evaluate the Answer Choices

(A) is correct, presenting the logical result of the Formal Logic based on the information given about the new system.

(B) is Out of Scope. There is nothing in the argument to support why the system wouldn't function properly.

(C) is a Distortion. Perhaps the ministry is absolutely concerned with productivity, but are misguided or unaware that their decision to maintain existing ways of working won't increase productivity, despite the new computer system. Alternatively, perhaps the ministry feels that employees are already working at peak productivity and there's just no reason to change that.

(D) is Out of Scope. The author makes no argument about whether the system would be worthwhile or not, and there's no information to support switching processes from manual to automated.

(E) is Out of Scope. The author's argument revolves on what's necessary for the system to increase efficiency. The ease of using the system is of no concern to the author.

15. (A) Flaw

Step 1: Identify the Question Type

The correct answer will described how the argument is "vulnerable to criticism," a common indication of a Flaw question.

Step 2: Untangle the Stimulus

The columnist concludes ([*s*]*o*) that car manufacturers are probably exaggerating their cars' normal fuel economy. This is based on the relatively weak fuel performance of the three cars owned by the columnist.

Step 3: Make a Prediction

There are two potential problems. The first is that the advertised fuel economy is said to occur "under normal driving conditions." Perhaps the columnist drives in abnormal conditions. However, even assuming the columnist does drive under normal conditions, the conclusion about cars in general is based on what happened with just three cars. That is far too small a sample size, making this a direct test of the flaw of representativeness.

Step 4: Evaluate the Answer Choices

(A) is correct, identifying the commonly tested flaw of using a potentially unrepresentative sample.

(B) is Extreme. The columnist doesn't have to assume *every* region has the same driving conditions. Some regions can have unusual conditions, and that would have no effect on the columnist's argument.

(C) is a 180. The columnist is accusing the manufacturers of being unreliable, not overlooking that possibility.

(D) is a Distortion. The author might be accusing manufacturers of knowingly inflating the fuel economy numbers, but that doesn't mean the cars fail to meet efficiency standards. They could be well above standards, but the manufacturers just market them as even *better*.

(E) is not accurate. The meaning of fuel economy does not change in the argument. It refers to the distance a car will travel given a certain amount of fuel (e.g., the commonly advertised "miles per gallon").

16. (C) Weaken

Step 1: Identify the Question Type
The question directly asks for something that "weakens the argument," making this a Weaken question.

Step 2: Untangle the Stimulus
According to the author, tenants don't have an incentive to conserve electricity when they don't pay the electric bill. *Thus*, the author concludes that installing meters and making the tenants pay the electric bill will lead to energy conservation.

Step 3: Make a Prediction
The author's conclusion is a prediction. Predictions generally have the same assumption: nothing relevant is going to change that might affect the expected results. In this case, the author assumes that making tenants pay for the electricity is not going to lead to some overlooked situation that would actually make energy conversation *less* likely. The correct answer will point out a potential change that *could* prevent the predicted outcome.

Step 4: Evaluate the Answer Choices

(C) is correct. This suggests that making the tenants pay would take away a strong incentive from landlords. If they stop supplying tenants with energy efficient appliances, that could make the energy conservation situation worse, not better.

(A) is irrelevant, as it does not address what would happen if tenants *do* pay the electric bills and what effect any of this has on energy conservation.

(B) is potentially a 180. If people are educated about energy conservation, then it's even more likely they'd start

conserving energy more if they suddenly became responsible for paying the electric bill.

(D) is Out of Scope. The argument is not about the likelihood or feasibility of installing electric meters. The argument is about what would happen *if* they were installed, regardless of the cost.

(E) is also Out of Scope. Even if there are other ways to get people to conserve energy, that does not mean the author's plan won't work.

17. (D) Role of a Statement

Step 1: Identify the Question Type
The question stem presents a claim from the stimulus and asks for the role it plays in the argument, making this a Role of a Statement question.

Step 2: Untangle the Stimulus
Start by identifying the claim in question, which appears in the second sentence. Then, break down the argument. The author starts by negating a position, which is often the sign of a conclusion. Sure enough, the author's conclusion is that you can't have punishments be proportional to a crime's seriousness *and* give harsher punishments to repeat offenders. As evidence, the author indicates an implication of this ineffective plan: It suggests years-old actions are relevant to new offenses. In that, all actions would be considered relevant, and that would make the proportional punishment concept impossible to apply.

Step 3: Make a Prediction
The phrase "[i]t implies" indicates that the claim in question is an implication of a position. That position is the one the author calls *unsustainable*. The correct answer will identify the claim in question as an implication of a plan the author argues won't work.

Step 4: Evaluate the Answer Choices

(D) is correct. It is an implication (i.e., consequence) of the view the author rejects.

(A) is a Distortion. The claim in question is used to support the conclusion, but the author provides no "grounds to accept" that claim. The author just presents it as fact and expects the reader to accept it without evidence.

(B) is a 180. The position that implies the claim in question is being *rejected* by the author, not defended.

(C) is a Distortion. The conclusion is in the first sentence ("[t]he position . . . is unsustainable), and the author offers no evidence to support the claim in question.

(E) is a Distortion. The claim in question is merely part of a string of evidence, but there is no intermediate conclusion for which this claim provides support.

18. (D) Assumption (Necessary)

Step 1: Identify the Question Type
The question directly asks for an assumption, and one that is "required by" the argument. That makes this a Necessary Assumption question.

Step 2: Untangle the Stimulus
The blogger describes how the media has changed from focusing on objectivity to embracing partisan reporting. The blogger argues that this change is based on changing business strategies. In the past, newspapers had no serious rivals, so their biggest goal was to avoid being offensive.

Step 3: Make a Prediction
This is a case of Mismatched Concepts. If the goal of newspapers was to avoid being offensive, what does that have to do with being objective? The blogger must assume that objective reporting was considered inoffensive—at the very least, it's not as offensive as the partisan reporting that is more prominent in today's media with its newer business strategies.

Step 4: Evaluate the Answer Choices

(D) is correct, making the requisite connection between objective reporting and the likelihood of being offensive.

(A) is a Distortion. The argument is about the partisanship of the journalism and the reporting, not of the journalists themselves.

(B) is Out of Scope. The argument is about the standards used by journalists and what may or may not offend readers. That's not necessarily the same as the preferences of readers. Objectivity may be less preferred, but also less offensive.

(C) is Out of Scope. The argument is not about how popular the media is. It's about the change in style from objective to partisan, and whether that's based on a change in views regarding offending readers.

(E) is Extreme and a 180. The blogger does not argue that there is *no* basis for being objective. If anything, the author presents a basis used in the past: trying to avoid offending the reader.

19. (C) Inference

Step 1: Identify the Question Type
The question asks for something that can be "properly inferred" from the statements provided, making this an Inference question.

Step 2: Untangle the Stimulus
The author begins with a piece of Formal Logic: A government practice that could lead to abuse of power should not be performed unless there's a compelling reason to do so. The author provides an example of keeping secrets, which can be justified. However, when the reasons are not compelling or when even the existence of the secret is not revealed, that can lead to an abuse of power.

Step 3: Make a Prediction
It helps to translate the opening Formal Logic and its contrapositive.

$$\text{If} \quad \begin{array}{c}\textit{undertake practice}\\ \textit{that could lead to abuse}\end{array} \rightarrow \textit{compelling reason}$$

$$\text{If} \sim \textit{compelling reason} \rightarrow \begin{array}{c}\sim \textit{undertake practice}\\ \textit{that could lead to abuse}\end{array}$$

The author claims that keeping secrets can be justified, in which case there *must* be a compelling reason for doing so. However, the author then says secrets are often kept for insubstantial reasons, in which cases it is *not* justified to keep those secrets. The author also says that concealing the existence of a secret could also lead to abuse of power. Again, by the logic, there would need to be a compelling reason for concealing that fact. Otherwise, there's no justification.

Step 4: Evaluate the Answer Choices

(C) is supported. By the statements, concealing a secret could lead to abuse of power, and the logic dictates such action should not be undertaken unless there's a compelling reason.

(A) is Extreme. If the act is not justified, it's probably because there's no compelling reason to do it. However, there's no indication that this happens in *most* cases. At worst, the author says that insubstantial reasoning happens "too often," but that doesn't necessarily mean most of the time.

(B) is a Distortion. If there's a compelling reason to keep a secret, that just means the keeping of that secret may be justified. That doesn't mean it won't facilitate abuse of power.

(D) is Extreme. If they don't have a compelling reason to conceal information, then they should not conceal that information . . . *if* it would lead to abuse of power. However, there's no certainty that all such information absolutely *will* lead to an abuse of power.

(E) is a Distortion. The requirement for keeping a secret is that there's a compelling reason to do so. Even if keeping a secret does make it easier to abuse power, a compelling reason can override that concern.

20. (E) Assumption (Sufficient)

Step 1: Identify the Question Type
The phrase "if assumed" indicates the correct answer will be an assumption that guarantees the conclusion, making this a Sufficient Assumption question.

Step 2: Untangle the Stimulus

According to the author, some musicians embrace the theory that music is just sounds with no meaning. The author concludes ([*t*]*hus*) that their music does not conform to this theory, i.e., there is some meaning—it's not just a bunch of sounds. The evidence for this is that these musicians explain their intentions before performing.

Step 3: Make a Prediction

As with almost all arguments in Sufficient Assumption questions, this one rests on Mismatched Concepts. The conclusion implies that the songs have meaning, while the evidence merely talks about how the musicians explain their intentions. The assumption connects those concepts: Explaining the intentions indicates that the music has some meaning.

Step 4: Evaluate the Answer Choices

(E) is correct. If music with no meaning is not explained, then by contrapositive, if music *is* explained, it must have meaning, confirming the author's argument.

(A) is Out of Scope. The ability to think symbolically has nothing to do with the author's argument. Also, the argument is focused on whether or not the music has meaning at all, not how *difficult* it is to create music with meaning.

(B) is a Distortion. The author claims that musicians "encourage audience acceptance," but that doesn't mean acceptance is necessary for music to have no meaning. In fact, the musicians probably believe their music has no meaning with or without audience acceptance.

(C) is a Distortion. This combines a lot of ideas from the argument (e.g., random series of sounds, meaning, audience acceptance). However, this only indicates what would make some music appealing. This does not verify the author's conclusion about whether or not music does have meaning.

(D) is a Distortion. The argument is not about whether or not people will enjoy the music. The argument is focused on whether or not the music has meaning.

21. (C) Method of Argument

Step 1: Identify the Question Type

The question asks for the author's "technique of reasoning," making this a Method of Argument question.

Step 2: Untangle the Stimulus

The author starts off by arguing that evolution does not always maximize the potential for survival. The rest of the argument is an extended example of moose, which evolved larger antlers to better fight off competition, but also makes them more visible and vulnerable to predators.

Step 3: Make a Prediction

The bulk of the argument is an example used to show how evolution does not always improve the survival rate of an

organism. The correct answer will describe this technique of countering an idea via example.

Step 4: Evaluate the Answer Choices

(C) is correct. The author challenges the idea that evolution is all about survival by presenting the counterexample of moose and their antlers.

(A) is Out of Scope. The author is countering a general idea about evolution, but there is no specific competing argument that the author is attacking.

(B) is a Distortion. An analogy is used when an author compares one specific circumstance to a different but similar specific circumstance. However, the author only raises one specific circumstance to address a general claim. That's an example or counterexample, not an analogy.

(D) is a Distortion. The example raised is about moose, and it's entirely relevant to the discussion of evolution. The author would not dispute her own example.

(E) is a Distortion. The author uses an example to undermine a claim, but the claim is not shown to be self-contradictory. In fact, the claim (evolution supports survival) may be just fine in some circumstances, just not in the moose example.

22. (D) Weaken

Step 1: Identify the Question Type

The question directly asks for something that "weakens the biologist's argument," making this a Weaken question.

Step 2: Untangle the Stimulus

The biologist describes how, when exposed to various colors of light, a particular species of bacteria gravitates toward a shade of red, a light color that aids its chlorophyll in producing energy. The biologist concludes that the bacteria detect the red color by monitoring its energy levels.

Step 3: Make a Prediction

The biologist is committing a correlation vs. causation flaw. There is a correlation between energy levels and the red color, but the biologist assumes the increased energy potential is what's causing the bacteria to move toward the red light. This could be weakened by showing an alternative explanation (i.e., they are moving toward the red light for a different reason) or by showing that it's just a coincidence (i.e., the energy level has no effect on which color is chosen).

Step 4: Evaluate the Answer Choices

(D) is correct. If blue would spur an equal level of energy creation, that suggests there's another reason the bacteria are gravitating toward red only.

(A) is a 180. If the bacteria stop gravitating toward red when they don't have chlorophyll, that suggests the energy produced by chlorophyll does indeed influence the bacteria's behavior, confirming rather than weakening the biologist's assertion.

(B) is also a 180. This suggests the bacteria are seeking out maximum energy production, which only confirms the biologist's argument.

(C) is yet another strengthener. If the red area *was* warmer, that might be an alternative explanation for the bacteria's behavior. However, if the temperature is the same, as this choice suggests, then warmth is not a factor, making it more likely the biologist's claim is correct.

(E) is an Irrelevant Comparison. There's no indication here why other bacteria gravitate toward other colors. Perhaps they contain some other substance that produces energy better under other colors. In that case, that would confirm, not weaken, the biologist's claim that energy production is a major factor.

23. (B) Flaw

Step 1: Identify the Question Type
The question directly asks for an answer that describes the flaw of the argument.

Step 2: Untangle the Stimulus
The argument begins with Formal Logic: If legislation is the product of groups negotiating and compromising, then none of those groups will be satisfied. The author then concludes that, because all of the groups involved in the new trade agreement are unsatisfied, compromises must have been made.

Step 3: Make a Prediction
Formal Logic in a Flaw question? The flaw of necessity vs. sufficiency is highly probable. Sure enough, in this argument, the Formal Logic dictates that compromise is sufficient to guarantee unhappy participants.

$$If \quad compromise \quad \rightarrow \quad unhappy\ participants$$

The author then concludes that the presence of unhappy groups indicates there must have been compromises, suggesting that compromise is a necessary condition for producing unhappy parties.

$$If \quad unhappy\ participants \quad \rightarrow \quad compromise$$

That is not logically sound, and the correct answer will describe this commonly tested flaw.

Step 4: Evaluate the Answer Choices
(B) is correct. The author concludes that comprise was necessary (i.e., it must have happened) for a result (i.e.,

unhappy groups) merely from the claim that compromise leads to unhappy groups. The groups could have been unhappy for many other reasons.

(A) is a Distortion. The conclusion doesn't merely restate the evidence. It gets the logic of the evidence backward.

(C) is not accurate. This suggests the flaw of equivocation, but all terms in the argument are used consistently and never change meaning.

(D) is Extreme. The author only argues that legislation involving compromises will ensure unhappy parties. However, if there's no need for compromise, then it's possible for all parties to be satisfied. The author never assumes otherwise.

(E) is a Distortion. A trade agreement would be a piece of legislation, and there's nothing about the trade agreement that would suggest it doesn't apply to the principle at hand.

24. (B) Inference

Step 1: Identify the Question Type
The correct answer will be "strongly supported by the information" given, making this an Inference question.

Step 2: Untangle the Stimulus
Following an accident at a power plant, researchers found three radioactive isotopes (call them I, Te, and Cs), but no heavy isotopes. There are only two possible sources: spent fuel rods or the plant's core. However, isotope Te is never found in spent fuel rods (in significant quantities), and radioactive material released directly from the core would have contained heavy isotopes. So where are isotopes I, Te, and Cs coming from? The author provides one more clue: Steam was released that may have contacted the core, even though it can easily dissolve those three radioactive isotopes.

Step 3: Make a Prediction
The key here is not to get too caught up in the scientific terms. In simple terms, researchers found three chemical items in the air. One possible source? Fuel rods. But fuel rods don't contain one of the chemicals in significant quantities. That leaves the other possible source: the core. However, if they came from the core directly, there would also have been heavy isotopes. So, they must have been released *indirectly*. And that's where the steam comes in. The chemicals must have escaped from the core indirectly through the steam.

Step 4: Evaluate the Answer Choices
(B) is supported. With only two possible sources (spent fuel rods or the core) and one source eliminated (spent fuel rods don't contain enough Te), the chemicals must have come from the second source: the core. And they wouldn't be ejected directly, so they must have taken an indirect route: the steam.

(A) is a Distortion. Because direct ejection would have included heavy isotopes, it's suggested that Te (and the other non-heavy isotopes) was ejected indirectly. However, if direct ejection *had* occurred, there's no reason to believe Te wouldn't have appeared then, too.

(C) is not supported. The spent fuel rods couldn't be the source of the Te, but they still could have been broken.

(D) is Out of Scope. The author implies that the material found did *not* come from spent fuel rods or directly from the core. While it's possible that other items were found that came from these sources, there's nothing in the statements that suggest as such.

(E) is not supported. It's only stated that the spent fuel rods do not contain Te, but there's no indication what they do contain, whether it be a lot of other heavy isotopes or not.

25. (E) Parallel Reasoning

Step 1: Identify the Question Type
The correct answer will be a complete argument with reasoning "most similar" to that in the argument given. That makes this a Parallel Reasoning question.

Step 2: Untangle the Stimulus
The argument given is based on some basic Formal Logic. If two sciences (ecology and physics) were evaluated equally, ecology would not be a successful science.

If	**evaluated by same criteria**	→	**ecology fails**

However, it *is* successful. Therefore, the author concludes that the two sciences are *not* evaluated equally.

If	**ecology ~ fail**	→	**~ evaluated by same criteria**

Step 3: Make a Prediction
The argument presents a piece of Formal Logic and then reaches its conclusion by using the contrapositive. In generic terms, the argument is structured as so: If X were true, then Y would be true. However Y is *not* true, so X is not true. The correct answer will conform to this exact same structure.

Step 4: Evaluate the Answer Choices
(E) is correct, using the same argument-by-contrapositive structure. If any economic theory were adequate, accurate forecasts could be made. Accurate forecasts *can't* be made, so economic theories are *not* adequate.

If	**adequate description**	→	**accurate economic forecasts**

If	**~ accurate economic forecasts**	→	**~ adequate description**

(A) does not match. Here, there are two consequences (connected by *or*) if taxes increase. One of those consequences can't happen, so the author concludes the other one must. However, there's no indication that the condition of a sales tax increase will happen. There's also no use of the contrapositive. And, the conclusion is a prediction, which is something the original author never makes.

(B) does not match. The Formal Logic here is: If the gallery borrows some works, then its exhibit would be the largest ever. However, unlike the original argument, this argument shifts to new topics such as the demand for larger exhibits and the willingness of galleries to lend out their works. Plus, the conclusion is a prediction, which does not match the conclusion of the original argument.

(C) does not match. This simply applies the Formal Logic as it is written without using the contrapositive. In generic terms, it says: If X were true, Y would be true. X will be true, so Y will be true, too. While the logic is sound, it does not match the original. Further, it makes a prediction, which is not logically equivalent to the original argument.

(D) does not match, and it commits a logical flaw. It simply negates the Formal Logic without reversing it. In generic terms, this is saying: If X were true, Y would be true. However, X is not usually true, so Y is not usually true. That's not logically sound, and it does not match the structure of the original argument.

Section IV: Logic Games
Game 1: Rural and Urban Photo Essays

Q#	Question Type	Correct	Difficulty
1	Partial Acceptability	E	Check your online resources.
2	Could Be True	B	Check your online resources.
3	"If" / Could Be True EXCEPT	C	Check your online resources.
4	Must Be True	D	Check your online resources.
5	Could Be True EXCEPT	A	Check your online resources.
6	Rule Substitution	B	Check your online resources.

Game 2: Concert Musicians

Q#	Question Type	Correct	Difficulty
7	Could Be True	D	Check your online resources.
8	"If" / Could Be True EXCEPT	A	Check your online resources.
9	Must Be False (CANNOT Be True)	E	Check your online resources.
10	"If" / Must Be False (CANNOT Be True)	D	Check your online resources.
11	Completely Determine	E	Check your online resources.

Game 3: Amusement Center Obstacle Course

Q#	Question Type	Correct	Difficulty
12	Acceptability	D	Check your online resources.
13	"If" / Must Be True	C	Check your online resources.
14	Complete and Accurate List	B	Check your online resources.
15	"If" / Must Be True	B	Check your online resources.
16	"If" / Must Be True	A	Check your online resources.

Game 4: Managers in Manila, Sydney, and Tokyo

Q#	Question Type	Correct	Difficulty
17	Acceptability	C	Check your online resources.
18	Completely Determine	B	Check your online resources.
19	Must Be True	D	Check your online resources.
20	Could Be True	A	Check your online resources.
21	"If" / Must Be True	D	Check your online resources.
22	"If" / Could Be True	A	Check your online resources.
23	Rule Substitution	E	Check your online resources.

Game 1: Rural and Urban Photo Essays

Step 1: Overview

Situation: A magazine assigning photo essays for upcoming issues

Entities: Five photographers (Fetter, Gonzalez, Howland, Jordt, Kim) and two themes (rural and urban)

Action: Sequencing/Matching Hybrid. Determine the order in which each photographer's essay will appear (Sequencing), and determine the theme of each photographer's essay (Matching).

Limitations: Each essay is assigned to a different photographer, making the sequencing standard one-to-one sequencing. For the matching, three essays will be rural and two will be urban.

Step 2: Sketch

Draw two rows of five slots labeled 1 through 5. The top row will be used to determine the order of the photographers, so list them by initial next to that row. The bottom row will be used to determine the theme, so draw three r's and two u's next to that row.

```
    1   2   3   4   5
   __  __  __  __  __      F G H J K
   __  __  __  __  __      r r r u u
```

You could also draw a single row of slots and use the top of each slot for the photographer and the bottom of each slot for the theme.

Step 3: Rules

Rule 1 establishes the first essay as rural. Draw "r" in slot 1 of the bottom row, and cross one "r" off the list next to that row.

Rule 2 creates a Block of Entities. Kim and Fetter, in that order, will be consecutive.

Rule 3 dictates that Fetter and Kim have different themes. Either make a note to the side for now, or somehow notate it under the block from the previous rule. Perhaps "x" under one and "y" under the other, or "r/u" under one and "u/r" under the other, with a note that they are different.

Rule 4 assigns Gonzalez to the third essay. Draw "G" in slot 3 of the top row, and cross "G" off the list next to that row.

Rule 5 establishes that the theme for Jordt's essay is urban.

Step 4: Deductions

Numbers are important in this game. Three photographers will have rural themes, while only two have urban themes. By Rule 3, Fetter and Kim have different themes, so one of them must have a rural theme and the other will have an urban theme. So, either Fetter or Kim gets one of the two urban themes and, by Rule 5, Jordt gets the other. The remaining photographers, Gonzalez and Howland, must then have rural themes, along with either Fetter or Kim (whoever doesn't get the urban theme).

At this point, an "r" can be placed under the "G" in essay 3. Then there's the Block of Kim and Fetter. With the Established Entity of Gonzalez taking up the third essay, Kim and Fetter could only be assigned essays 1 and 2, respectively, or essays 4 and 5, respectively. These two outcomes would each establish three of the five photographers, suggesting Limited Options are worthwhile.

In the first option, Kim and Fetter are assigned to essays 1 and 2, respectively. Essay 1 is already established as rural, so essay 2 for Fetter will be urban. Howland and Jordt will be assigned to essays 4 and 5, in either order. Note that Howland's essay will be rural and Jordt's essay will be urban.

```
I)   1    2    3    4     5      ┌───┐ ┌───┐
     K    F    G   H/J   J/H     │ H │ │ J │
     r    u    r   __    __      │ r │ │ u │
                                 └───┘ └───┘
```

In the second option, Kim and Fetter are assigned to essays 4 and 5, respectively. It cannot be determined which one will be rural and which one will be urban. However, that leaves Howland and Jordt for essays 1 and 2. Essay 1 is rural and Jordt has to have an urban theme. So, Howland must be assigned to essay 1, and Jordt to essay 2.

```
II)  1    2    3    4      5
     H    J    G    K      F
     r    u    r   r/u ≠ u/r
```

Step 5: Questions

1. (E) Partial Acceptability

Start by using standard Acceptability tactics. Go through the rules one at a time and eliminate choices that violate those rules. Because the choices don't list the essay themes, some rules may have to be tested indirectly or in combination with other rules.

With no themes listed, Rules 1, 3, and 5 cannot be tested directly. **(A)** and **(C)** violate Rule 2 by not having Kim and Fetter consecutive. **(B)** violates Rule 4 by putting Gonzalez first, not third.

Combining Rules 1 and 5, the first essay must be rural, so it cannot be Jordt's, which must be urban. **(D)** violates that, leaving **(E)** as the correct answer.

Note that Limited Options could have been used to save even more time. By the two options, the first essay has to be assigned to Howland or Kim. That immediately narrows the choices down to **(C)** and **(E)**, and **(C)** does not match the option with Howland first because it splits up Kim and Fetter.

2. (B) Could Be True

The correct answer will be the one that is possible. The four wrong choices will be impossible, i.e., must be false.

If Fetter's essay were immediately before Jordt's, that would create a three-person block of KFJ. With Gonzalez assigned the third essay, there would be no room for such a block. That eliminates **(A)**.

Gonzalez's essay is third. If Gonzalez's essay were immediately before Howland's, then Howland's essay would be fourth. That violates no rules and is even seen as possible in Option I. Thus, this could be true, making **(B)** correct. For the record:

If Howland's or Jordt's essay were immediately before Kim's, that would create a three-person block of either HKF or JKF. With Gonzalez assigned the third essay, there would be no room for either block. That eliminates **(C)** and **(D)**.

(E) directly contradicts Rule 2, which states that Kim's essay must be immediately before Fetter's, not Gonzalez's.

3. (C) "If" / Could Be True EXCEPT

For this question, the fourth issue will have an urban theme. This could happen in either option, so draw both out. In Option I, Kim, Fetter, and Gonzalez, in that order, are assigned to the first three essays with rural, urban, and rural themes, respectively. If the fourth essay is urban, then the fifth essay must be the final rural one. Jordt must have an urban theme, so Jordt is assigned to essay 4, leaving Howland for essay 5.

In Option II, the photographers are all determined. For this question, it's now established that essay 4 (Kim's) is urban, making essay 5 (Fetter's) rural.

	1	2	3	4	5
I)	K	F	G	J	H
	r	u	r	u	r
II)	H	J	G	K	F
	r	u	r	u	r

With that, these options show Howland's essay as first or fifth, never fourth. That makes **(C)** impossible and thus the correct answer. Each of the remaining choices are possible in one of the two options.

4. (D) Must Be True

The correct answer for this question must be true, which means the four wrong choices may not be, i.e., could be false.

Consider the major deductions. There are two urban themes. Jordt has one. And, because Kim and Fetter must have different themes, one of them has the other. That means the remaining photographers, Gonzalez and Howland, must have rural themes. That makes **(D)** definitively true, and thus the correct answer. For the record:

(A) is certainly false, as Gonzalez is assigned the third essay and Gonzalez gets a rural theme. The fifth essay could be rural, but it could also be urban. So, **(B)** could be false. And Fetter and Kim have different themes, but it's possible that Fetter has a rural theme and Kim has an urban theme. Thus, **(C)** and **(E)** could be false.

5. (A) Could Be True EXCEPT

Four choices here could be the fourth essay. That means the correct answer will be the exception: the one that cannot be, i.e., must be false.

Limited Options help out a lot here. In Option I, the fourth essay could be either Jordt's urban essay or Howland's rural essay. In Option II, the fourth essay will be Kim's, and could be either rural or urban. That sums up choices **(B)**, **(C)**, **(D)**, and **(E)**, which means those are the incorrect "could be true" choices. Further, it's impossible for the fourth essay to be Fetter's because Gonzalez's is third and Fetter has to come immediately after Kim, not Gonzalez. That makes **(A)** impossible and thus the correct answer.

6. (B) Rule Substitution

The correct answer here will be a new rule that could replace Rule 3, regarding Fetter and Kim having different themes, without affecting the game in any way. In other words, Rule 3 will be eliminated, and the correct answer has to re-establish that exact same restriction without adding any new restrictions.

Simply establishing Howland with a rural theme is not enough. With Rule 5, Jordt has an urban theme, but that still leaves two rural themes and one urban theme. That would allow Fetter and Kim to both have rural themes. Thus, **(A)** is not good enough.

However, if both Gonzalez *and* Howland are assigned rural themes, that would help. Then, Jordt gets an urban theme by Rule 5. That leaves one urban theme and one rural theme for Fetter and Kim. That would force them to have different themes, as the original rule did. And Gonzalez and Howard were always assigned rural themes originally, so there are no new restrictions. That makes **(B)** the correct answer. For the record:

(C) does not prevent Fetter and Kim from having the same theme, and it forces Fetter to have a rural theme, which was not always the case. **(D)** adds a restriction to Jordt's essay which happens to be true based on the deductions. However, it does nothing to prevent Kim and Fetter from having the same theme. **(E)** would actually have the complete opposite effect. If Kim's essay had the same theme as Gonzalez's or Howland's, but not both, then Gonzalez and Howland would have to have different themes. So, one of them would get an urban theme along with Jordt. That would leave only rural themes for Kim and Fetter, giving them both the *same* theme, not different.

Game 2: Concert Musicians

Step 1: Overview

Situation: Musicians performing at a concert

Entities: Seven musicians (Lowe, Miller, Nadel, Otero, Parker, Sen, Thomas)

Action: Strict Sequencing. Determine the order in which the musicians will perform. Although the first two rules are loose sequencing style rules, Rules 3, 4, and 5 make this a Strict Sequencing game.

Limitations: Each musician performs, one at a time. This is standard one-to-one sequencing.

Step 2: Sketch

List the musicians by initial and draw a series of seven consecutively numbered slots.

L M N O P S T

$$\frac{\quad}{1} \ \frac{\quad}{2} \ \frac{\quad}{3} \ \frac{\quad}{4} \ \frac{\quad}{5} \ \frac{\quad}{6} \ \frac{\quad}{7}$$

Step 3: Rules

Rules 1 and 2 set up two separate loose relationships: Lowe at some point before Nadel, and Miller at some point before Thomas.

L . . . N
M . . . T

Rules 3 and 4 set up two similar strict relationships. There is exactly one space between Lowe and Otero, and one space between Miller and Parker, though each pair can appear in either order.

$$\frac{L/O}{M/P} \ \_ \ \frac{O/L}{P/M}$$

Rule 5 presents two options. Parker will be first or seventh (i.e., last). You can draw "P" over the sketch with arrows pointing to the first and last spots. However, Parker's placement directly affects Miller's placement, and that will have other effects. So, drawing Limited Options might be a better course of action.

Step 4: Deductions

Based on the last rule, draw two sketches. In the first, Parker will be first. By Rule 4, Miller will be third. By Rule 2, Thomas must perform after Miller, so Thomas can be anywhere but second. Nadel also cannot be second, as Nadel must perform after Lowe (Rule 1). That means the second performer could be Lowe or Otero, which would mean Lowe and Otero take up positions two and four, with Miller in between. Or, the second performer could be Sen, the Floater of the game. Also,

because Lowe has to perform before Nadel, Lowe cannot perform last.

$$I) \quad \underset{1}{\overset{P}{\_}} \ \underset{2}{\_} \ \underset{3}{\overset{M}{\_}} \ \underset{4}{\_} \ \underset{5}{\_} \ \underset{6}{\_} \ \underset{7}{\_}$$
~T   ~L
~N

In the second option, Parker will be seventh. By Rule 4, Miller will be fifth. That means Thomas must be sixth (Rule 2). That leaves the first four slots open. The only definite order is that Lowe must perform before Nadel, so Lowe cannot be fourth and Nadel cannot be first. There's also the restriction about Lowe and Otero, but they could be in positions 1 and 3, or in positions 2 and 4 (as long as Otero is fourth).

$$II) \quad \underset{1}{\_} \ \underset{2}{\_} \ \underset{3}{\_} \ \underset{4}{\_} \ \underset{5}{\overset{M}{\_}} \ \underset{6}{\overset{T}{\_}} \ \underset{7}{\overset{P}{\_}}$$
~N   ~L

Step 5: Questions

7. (D) Could Be True

The correct answer will be the one that could be true. The remaining choices cannot be true, i.e., they must be false.

With Parker either first or seventh, Miller could only be third or fifth (Rule 4), never fourth. That eliminates **(A)**.

Nadel has to perform after Lowe, so can never be first. That eliminates **(B)**.

If Otero is fifth, then Miller can't be fifth, so Parker can't be seventh. Thus, Parker would be first and Miller third. This is Option I. If Otero is fifth, then Rule 3 requires Lowe to be third or seventh. However, in this option, Miller is third, and Lowe cannot be last without violating Rule 1. This is impossible, which eliminates **(C)**.

There is no rule directly restricting Sen—a Floater—so it would seem possible for Sen to perform seventh. In that case, Parker would have to perform first with Miller third, as seen in Option I. That leaves enough options for placing Lowe and Otero, as well as Nadel and Thomas. This is possible, making **(D)** correct. For the record:

If Thomas performed second, Miller would have to perform first (Rule 2). That would force Parker to perform third (Rule 4), violating Rule 5. That eliminates **(E)**.

8. (A) "If" / Could Be True EXCEPT

For this question, Otero performs earlier than Miller. This could happen in either option, so test them both. The correct answer will be the one person who cannot perform fifth. So, eliminate any musician who could perform fifth in either scenario.

In Option I, for Otero to be before Miller, Otero would have to perform second. In that case, Lowe would have to perform fourth (Rule 3). The remaining musicians, Nadel, Sen, and Thomas, could fill in the remaining positions in any order. So any of those three could be fifth, which eliminates **(C)**, **(D)**, and **(E)**.

$$\text{I)} \quad \underset{1}{P} \quad \underset{2}{O} \quad \underset{3}{M} \quad \underset{4}{L} \quad \underset{5}{\_\_} \quad \underset{6}{\_\_} \quad \underset{7}{\_\_}$$

N, S, T

In Option II, Otero is definitely before Miller and Miller is the fifth performer there. That eliminates **(B)**.

$$\text{II)} \quad \underset{1}{\_\_} \quad \underset{2}{\_\_} \quad \underset{3}{\_\_} \quad \underset{4}{\_\_} \quad \underset{5}{M} \quad \underset{6}{T} \quad \underset{7}{P}$$

That leaves **(A)** as the correct answer, as Lowe cannot be fifth in either outcome when Otero is before Miller.

9. (E) Must Be False (CANNOT Be True)

The correct answer will be a musician who cannot perform third, i.e., it must be false that musician is third. The remaining choices will list musicians who *could* perform third.

In Option I, Miller is third, so that eliminates **(B)**.

In Option II, Lowe, Nadel, Otero, and Sen occupy the first four slots, including the third performance. Lowe and Otero must be separated by one space. So, it's possible for Lowe and Otero to perform first and third, in either order, as long as Nadel performs after Lowe (e.g., fourth). So, Lowe and Otero could each perform third, eliminating **(A)** and **(D)**.

$$\text{II)} \quad \underset{1}{L/O} \quad \underset{2}{N/S} \quad \underset{3}{O/L} \quad \underset{4}{S/N} \quad \underset{5}{M} \quad \underset{6}{T} \quad \underset{7}{P}$$

L . . . N

The only other possibility in Option II is to have Lowe and Otero perform second and fourth. For Lowe to perform before Nadel, Lowe would have to be second with Nadel third. Nadel could be third, which eliminates **(C)**.

$$\text{II)} \quad \underset{1}{S} \quad \underset{2}{L} \quad \underset{3}{N} \quad \underset{4}{O} \quad \underset{5}{M} \quad \underset{6}{T} \quad \underset{7}{P}$$

Sen is the only musician who cannot perform third. Although Sen is not directly affected by the rules, placing Sen third would force the remaining musicians into positions that wind up violating the rules. Thus **(E)** is impossible, making it the correct answer.

10. (D) "If" / Must Be False (CANNOT Be True)

For this question, Sen and Thomas, in that order, are consecutive. If Parker were seventh, Miller would be fifth (Rule 4), forcing Thomas to be sixth (Rule 2), making it impossible for Sen and Thomas to be consecutive. So, this could only work in Option I, when Parker is first. In that case, Miller is third. The block of Sen and Thomas cannot fill the one space between Parker and Miller, and Nadel cannot perform second because Nadel has to perform after Lowe. That leaves two performers for the second slot: Lowe and Otero. If Lowe performs second, Otero would perform fourth, and vice versa. So, Lowe and Otero must be second and fourth, in either order.

$$\text{I)} \quad \underset{1}{P} \quad \underset{2}{L/O} \quad \underset{3}{M} \quad \underset{4}{O/L} \quad \underset{5}{\_\_} \quad \underset{6}{\_\_} \quad \underset{7}{\_\_}$$

That leaves the block of Sen and Thomas, in that order, to perform fifth and sixth, or sixth and seventh. Nadel will fill in the remaining spot.

$$\text{I)} \quad \underset{1}{P} \quad \underset{2}{L/O} \quad \underset{3}{M} \quad \underset{4}{O/L} \quad \underset{5}{S} \quad \underset{6}{T} \quad \underset{7}{N}$$

or

$$\text{I)} \quad \underset{1}{P} \quad \underset{2}{L/O} \quad \underset{3}{M} \quad \underset{4}{O/L} \quad \underset{5}{N} \quad \underset{6}{S} \quad \underset{7}{T}$$

With that, Thomas can only perform sixth or seventh, not fifth. That makes **(D)** impossible, and thus the correct answer.

11. (E) Completely Determine

The correct answer will place someone in such a way that all seven musicians can be placed with absolute certainty.

If Lowe performs fourth, Otero could still perform second or sixth, so there's still some uncertainty. That eliminates **(A)**.

If Miller performs fifth, Parker is seventh and Thomas is sixth. However, that's the setup for Option II, which still leaves a lot of uncertainty about the first four performances. That eliminates **(B)**.

If Nadel is fourth, Lowe must perform earlier. That could happen in Option II. However, in that case, Lowe could be first with Otero third, or Lowe could be third with Otero first. It's not completely determined, so that eliminates **(C)**.

If Otero is third, that could only happen in Option II with Miller fifth, Thomas sixth, and Parker seventh. Lowe would have to be first, but Nadel and Sen could then perform second and fourth in either order. That's two possible outcomes, not one. That eliminates **(D)**.

If Sen performs first, Parker must perform seventh. That means Miller performs fifth and Thomas sixth. That leaves Lowe, Nadel, and Otero for the second, third, and fourth performances. Lowe and Otero need to be separated, so Nadel must perform third, in between them. Lowe has to perform before Nadel, so Lowe must be second and Otero fourth. All seven musicians are assigned with certainty, making **(E)** the correct answer.

II) $\dfrac{S}{1} \quad \dfrac{L}{2} \quad \dfrac{N}{3} \quad \dfrac{O}{4} \quad \dfrac{M}{5} \quad \dfrac{T}{6} \quad \dfrac{P}{7}$

In a pinch, this seemed the most likely answer as it places Sen—the Floater—who was otherwise not directly restricted.

Game 3: Amusement Center Obstacle Course

Step 1: Overview

Situation: Amusement center operators designing an obstacle course

Entities: Six obstacles (rope bridge, spinning platform, tunnel, vaulting apparatus, wall, zipline)

Action: Strict Sequencing. Determine the order in which the obstacles will be placed. A quick glance at the rules reveals that they are all strict sequencing style rules.

Limitations: Each obstacle is included and separate, so this is standard one-to-one sequencing.

Step 2: Sketch

List the obstacles by initial and draw six consecutively numbered slots. (Note: You can use dual initials for the obstacles, e.g., "RB" for the rope bridge. However, just using the first initial of each obstacle is sufficient as they are distinct and presented alphabetically. Also, it can be less confusing to see six individual letters rather than a mixture of single- and double-letter items).

$$R \ S \ T \ V \ W \ Z$$
$$\underline{\quad} \ \underline{\quad} \ \underline{\quad} \ \underline{\quad} \ \underline{\quad} \ \underline{\quad}$$
$$1 \quad 2 \quad 3 \quad 4 \quad 5 \quad 6$$

Step 3: Rules

Rule 1 limits the spinning platform to one of two positions: third or fourth. Draw "S" above/below the sketch with arrows pointing to the third and fourth slot.

Rule 2 creates a Block of Entities with the wall and the zipline consecutive, in that order.

$$\boxed{W \ Z}$$

Rule 3 prevents the rope bridge and the vaulting apparatus from being consecutive, in either order.

$$\text{Never} \ \boxed{R \ V} \ \text{or} \ \boxed{V \ R}$$

Step 4: Deductions

By Rule 2, the wall must be before the zipline, so the wall cannot be last and the zipline cannot be first. It's also impossible to place the wall and zipline third and fourth, respectively, as that would leave no place for the spinning platform.

However, that leaves four possible placements for the wall/zipline block. With only five questions, it's not worth drawing out all four options.

It might seem tempting to set up Limited Options based on where the spinning platform goes. However, in either

position, there are still multiple places for the wall/zipline block that would also allow the rope bridge and vaulting apparatus to be separated. So, neither option would produce any fruitful deductions.

There are no Numbers deductions and no Duplication deductions. Deductions are rather sparse here. However, it's helpful to note that the tunnel is a Floater. Also, the game thankfully comes with a bunch of New-"If" questions, and that can often indicate a lack of major deductions. The final Master Sketch should reflect what's known so far:

$$\begin{array}{c} S \\ \swarrow \ \searrow \end{array}$$
$$\underline{\quad} \ \underline{\quad} \ \underline{\quad} \ \underline{\quad} \ \underline{\quad} \ \underline{\quad}$$
$$1 \quad 2 \quad 3 \quad 4 \quad 5 \quad 6$$
$$\sim Z \quad\quad \sim W \ \sim Z \quad\quad \sim W$$

Step 5: Questions

12. (D) Acceptability

As with any Acceptability question, go through the rules one at a time and eliminate answers that violate them.

(C) violates Rule 1 by putting the spinning platform fifth.**(A)** violates Rule 2 by separating the wall and the zipline. **(B)** and **(E)** violate Rule 3 by having the rope bridge and vaulting apparatus consecutive. That leaves **(D)** as the correct answer.

13. (C) "If" / Must Be True

For this question, the tunnel will be first. The spinning platform could still go third or fourth, so test them both.

If the spinning platform is third, the wall/zipline block would have to go after, either in 4/5 or 5/6—so no matter what one of the wall/zipline block will occupy slot 5. That leaves either the rope bridge or the vaulting apparatus for the second obstacle.

$$\begin{array}{cccccc} T & R/V & S & \underline{\quad} & W/Z & \underline{\quad} \\ 1 & 2 & 3 & 4 & 5 & 6 \end{array}$$

If the spinning platform is fourth, that leaves two sets of spaces for the wall/zipline block: second and third, or fifth and sixth. However, in either case, that would leave consecutive spaces for the rope bridge and the vaulting apparatus, violating Rule 3. This option is unacceptable.

$$\begin{array}{cccccc} T & \underline{\quad} & \underline{\quad} & S & \underline{\quad} & \underline{\quad} \\ 1 & 2 & 3 & 4 & 5 & 6 \end{array}$$
$$\boxed{W \ Z}$$

So, if the tunnel is first, the spinning platform can only be third, making **(C)** the correct answer. The remaining answers are all possible, but need not be true.

14. (B) Complete and Accurate List

The correct answer will list every possible position for the tunnel. The wrong choices will leave something out or include a position where the tunnel cannot go.

Answering this question efficiently would require finding a very challenging deduction at the beginning. Without that, this question is worth skipping and saving for last. Using sketches and outcomes from other questions can save a lot of testing. The answer to the Acceptability question shows that the tunnel can be second, and the second question of the set is based on the possibility that the tunnel can be first. Unfortunately, every answer lists those positions, so that doesn't help. However, the sketch for the last question places the tunnel sixth, so that eliminates **(A)**, which fails to list sixth.

From there, without an incredible deduction, it's all about testing. Start by testing whether the tunnel could be third. If it were, then the spinning platform would be fourth. That leaves two sets of open spaces: first and second, and fifth and sixth.

However, this cannot happen. The wall/zipline block would have to take up one set of spaces, leaving the rope bridge and the vaulting apparatus to be consecutive in the other set of spaces. This violates Rule 3 and is thus unacceptable. So, **(C)**, **(D)**, and **(E)** can all be eliminated for including the impossible position of third.

At this point, **(B)** is the only answer left and is thus correct. For the record, the tunnel cannot be fourth because that would make the spinning platform third, leading to the same problem as placing the tunnel third. You could draw one more sketch to prove that the tunnel could be fifth, but that's not necessary as all of the remaining choices have been eliminated.

15. (B) "If" / Must Be True

For this question, the rope bridge is second. That means the vaulting apparatus cannot be first or third. The first obstacle also cannot be the spinning platform, nor can it include the wall/zipline block. That leaves the tunnel as the first obstacle. That makes **(B)** the correct answer.

The remaining answers are either completely false or are possible, but not definitively true.

16. (A) "If" / Must Be True

For this question, the rope bridge and the vaulting apparatus are both earlier than the tunnel. The rope bridge and the vaulting apparatus cannot be next to one another, so there must be at least one other obstacle before the tunnel. Thus, the tunnel cannot be first, second, or third. It must be fourth, fifth, or sixth, leaving no room after it for the spinning platform. Thus, the spinning platform must also be before the tunnel.

That leaves the wall/zipline block. If that came after the tunnel, the tunnel would be fourth, making the spinning platform third, which would force the rope bridge and the vaulting apparatus to be consecutive, violating Rule 3.

So, the wall/zipline block must also be before the tunnel. That's everything, which means the tunnel must be last. Next, consider the spinning platform. If the spinning platform were third, that would create two sets of spaces: first and second, and fourth and fifth. The wall/zipline block would take one set, but that would again force the rope bridge and the vaulting apparatus to be consecutive. That can't happen, so the spinning platform must be fourth. That makes **(A)** the correct answer. The wall/zipline block will either go first/second or second/third. One of the rope bridge or vaulting apparatus will be fifth with the other one either first or third.

(B), **(C)**, **(D)**, and **(E)**, are either completely false or are possible, but not definitively true.

Game 4: Managers in Manila, Sydney, and Tokyo

Step 1: Overview

Situation: A company sending product managers to visit some cities

Entities: Four managers (Fan, Gleeson, Haley, Ibañez) and three cities (Manila, Sydney, Tokyo)

Action: Matching. Determine which managers are assigned to each city.

Limitations: Each manager is assigned at least once, and two managers are assigned to each city. That's a total of six assignments for four managers, so either one manager goes to all three cities or two managers go to two cities each.

Step 2: Sketch

List the managers by initial and set up a table with the three cities as column headings. Draw two slots under each column.

```
      F G H I
  Man  Syd  Tok
  ___ | ___ | ___
  ___ | ___ | ___
```

Step 3: Rules

Rule 1 sets up a Numeric Restriction. Ibañez goes to exactly two cities. Draw a second "I" in the entity list. You could also make a note to the side (e.g., "Exactly 2 I's").

Rule 2 prevents Fan and Haley from visiting the same city.

```
Never | F
      | H
```

Rule 3 provides some Formal Logic. If Gleeson goes to Manila, Haley goes to Tokyo. By contrapositive, if Haley does not go to Tokyo, then Gleeson cannot go to Manila.

$$\frac{Man}{G} \rightarrow \frac{Tok}{H}$$

$$\sim\frac{Tok}{H} \rightarrow \sim\frac{Man}{G}$$

Rule 4 prevents Gleeson from going to Sydney. Draw "~G" under the Sydney column.

Step 4: Deductions

Gleeson is duplicated in the last two rules. Gleeson cannot visit Sydney, which leaves Manila and Tokyo. The key question is if Gleeson visits Manila. If Gleeson does visit Manila, that triggers the Formal Logic of Rule 3. If Gleeson does *not* visit Manila, then she must visit Tokyo. Either way, some valuable deductions can be made. It is worth setting up Limited Options.

In the first option, Gleeson visits Manila. In that case, Haley vists Tokyo. That means Fan cannot visit Tokyo (Rule 2). That leaves one of Gleeson and Ibañez to be the second manager in Tokyo. Note that in Option I, Gleeson can still visit Tokyo, as managers can be sent to multiple cities.

```
I)  Man   Syd   Tok
     G    ___    H
    ___   ___   G/I
          ~G    ~F
```

In the second option, Gleeson does not visit Manila. In that case, she must visit Tokyo.

```
II)  Man   Syd   Tok
    ___   ___    G
    ___   ___   ___
    ~G    ~G
```

At this point, Numbers become important. Each city will be visited by two managers. In both options, there's at least one city that cannot be visited by Gleeson (Sydney in Option I, Manila and Sydney in Option II). In each case, that leaves Fan, Haley and Ibañez. However, Fan and Haley cannot be together (Rule 2). So, each of those cities can only get one of Fan or Haley, and the second manager must be Ibañez.

There's one final Numbers deduction to note. Ibañez must visit exactly two cities. This affects Option II, as Ibañez is already assigned twice and can no longer be assigned to Tokyo. So, the last spot in Tokyo must go to Fan or Haley.

```
I)  Man   Syd   Tok
     G     I     H
    ___   F/H   G/I

II)  Man   Syd   Tok
      I     I     G
     F/H   F/H   F/H
```

Further, if Ibañez goes to two cities and each other employee goes to one, that would be a total of five assignments. However, there are six slots, so exactly one other employee must be assigned to a second city.

Step 5: Questions

17. (C) Acceptability

This is a typical Acceptability question. Test each rule, one at a time, and eliminate answers that violate those rules.

(A) violates Rule 1 by assigning Ibañez to just one city.

(E) violates Rule 2 by assigning Fan and Haley together to Tokyo. **(D)** violates Rule 3 by assigning Gleeson to Manila without assigning Haley to Tokyo. **(B)** violates Rule 4 by assigning Gleeson to Sydney. That leaves **(C)** as the correct answer.

18. (B) Completely Determine

The correct answer will establish a condition that will allow all six assignments to be determined with no uncertainty. Eliminate any choice that allows for more than one outcome.

Fan can visit any pair of cities, as long as Haley visits the third. Similarly, Haley can visit any pair of cities, as long as Fan visits the third. However, in either case, it's not certain which cities are visited by whom. That eliminates **(A)** and **(C)**.

If Gleeson visits two cities, they could only be Manila and Tokyo (Rule 4). With Gleeson in Manila, Haley must visit Tokyo (Rule 3). With Tokyo filled, Ibañez still needs to visit two cities. They must be Manila and Sydney. That leaves one slot in Sydney, which must be taken up by Fan, who has nowhere else left to go. The entire outcome is determined, making **(B)** the correct answer.

$$
\begin{array}{c|c|c|c}
\text{I)} & \text{Man} & \text{Syd} & \text{Tok} \\
\hline
& G & I & H \\
& I & F & G \\
\end{array}
$$

For the record: If Fan and Gleeson visit Tokyo, Ibañez would be left with Manila and Sydney. Haley could visit Manila or Sydney, or both. With multiple possibilities, that eliminates **(D)**.

If Gleeson and Haley visit Tokyo, Ibañez would be left with Manila and Sydney. Fan could visit Manila or Sydney, or both. With multiple possibilities, that eliminates **(E)**.

19. (D) Must Be True

The correct answer has to be true no matter what. The wrong choices could be false or are definitely false.

In both options, Gleeson cannot visit Sydney. Fan and Haley cannot both visit Sydney, so only one of them can. The second manager visiting Sydney must be Ibañez, making **(D)** the correct answer.

20. (A) Could Be True

The correct answer to this question is the only one that could be true. The remaining choices will all be impossible, i.e., must be false.

In Option II, it is possible for Fan and Ibañez to visit Manila together. That makes **(A)** the correct answer. For the record:

Gleeson cannot visit Sydney, so Ibañez must visit Sydney to prevent Fan and Haley from being together. If Gleeson and Ibañez visit Tokyo, that would be Ibañez's second city. That would leave Fan, Gleeson, and Haley to visit Manila. However, without Haley in Tokyo, Gleeson cannot visit Manila.

And without Gleeson, that would leave Fan and Haley together, violating Rule 2. This ultimately is impossible, which eliminates **(B)**.

Ibañez has to visit Sydney, but can only visit two cities. Thus, Ibañez cannot visit Manila and Tokyo, too. That eliminates **(C)**.

Neither Fan nor Haley can visit three cities. With Ibañez visiting two cities, that would mean Fan or Haley visits three cities, Ibañez visits two, and one other manager visits one city. Somebody would be left out. That eliminates **(D)** and **(E)**.

21. (D) "If" / Must Be True

For this question, Gleeson and Haley visit a city together. Gleeson cannot visit Sydney, so it must be Manila or Tokyo.

If Gleeson and Haley visit Manila together, Haley must also visit Tokyo (Rule 3). Ibañez would then be left to visit Sydney and Tokyo. That would leave only Sydney for Fan.

$$
\begin{array}{c|c|c}
\text{Man} & \text{Syd} & \text{Tok} \\
\hline
G & I & H \\
H & F & I \\
\end{array}
$$

If Gleeson and Haley visit Tokyo together, Ibañez would be left to visit Manila and Sydney. Fan could visit Manila, Sydney, or both.

$$
\begin{array}{c|c|c}
\text{Man} & \text{Syd} & \text{Tok} \\
\hline
I & I & G \\
& & H \\
\hline
& \nwarrow F \nearrow & \\
\end{array}
$$

In either case, Haley visits Tokyo, making **(D)** the correct answer. The remaining choices are all possible, but need not be true.

22. (A) "If" / Could Be True

For this question, Ibañez visits Tokyo (which can only happen in Option I). If you haven't made Limited Options though and need to start from scratch, Ibañez also must visit Sydney because Gleeson cannot visit Sydney and Fan and Haley cannot visit a city together.

With Ibañez done, that leaves Manila open to Fan, Gleeson, and Haley. Again, Fan and Haley cannot visit there together. So, only one of them can visit Manila, and Gleeson must be the second manager. With Gleeson visiting Manila, Haley must visit Tokyo.

$$
\begin{array}{c|c|c}
\text{Man} & \text{Syd} & \text{Tok} \\
\hline
G & I & H \\
F/H & F/H & I \\
\end{array}
$$

With that, only **(A)** is possible, and is thus the correct answer. Ibañez cannot visit Manila in this case, and must visit Sydney and Tokyo, eliminating **(B)** and **(C)**. With both Haley and Ibañez in Tokyo, there's no room for Fan, which eliminates **(D)**. As for **(E)**, Haley could go to Manila or Sydney, but if she went to both, there'd be no city left for Fan to visit, so **(E)** is eliminated.

23. (E) Rule Substitution
For this question, Rule 2 is removed from the setup. The correct answer will provide a new condition that replicates all of the effects of Rule 2 (i.e., splitting up Fan and Haley) without adding any new restrictions.

The original restrictions did not require Gleeson and Ibañez to be split up. Also, that would not keep Fan and Haley apart. Thus, **(A)** is eliminated.

Haley was never required to visit Tokyo if Fan visits Sydney. And if Haley did have to visit Tokyo in that case, it wouldn't stop Haley from also visiting Sydney with Fan. **(B)** does not work and can be eliminated.

Restricting Fan and Haley from being together in Tokyo would not prevent them from being together in other cities. That eliminates **(C)**.

(D) sets up some clever Formal Logic. If Fan does not go to a particular city, then Haley must. However, that was not always the case. It was possible in the original for a city to not have Fan, but also not have Haley. In that case, the city could have Gleeson and Ibañez. This Formal Logic would be restrictive in a way the original rules were not, which makes **(D)** incorrect.

(E) also has some clever Formal Logic, but it works. By this rule, a city without Ibañez would have to be visited by Gleeson. By contrapositive, if a city did not have Gleeson, it must have Ibañez. In short, if one of them isn't there, the other one is, i.e., each city has to be visited by at least one of them. It's possible to have both, but you can't get rid of both Gleeson and Ibañez. By doing that, it prevents Fan and Haley from being together, establishing the original rule. And this was always true with the original rule, because splitting up Fan and Haley made it necessary to include Gleeson or Ibañez (or both) in each city. The original conditions are restored, and no new restrictions are added. That makes **(E)** the correct answer.

Glossary

Logical Reasoning

Logical Reasoning Question Types

Argument-Based Questions

Main Point Question

A question that asks for an argument's conclusion or an author's main point. Typical question stems:

> Which one the following most accurately expresses the conclusion of the argument as a whole?

> Which one of the following sentences best expresses the main point of the scientist's argument?

Role of a Statement Question

A question that asks how a specific sentence, statement, or idea functions within an argument. Typical question stems:

> Which one of the following most accurately describes the role played in the argument by the statement that automation within the steel industry allowed steel mills to produce more steel with fewer workers?

> The claim that governmental transparency is a nation's primary defense against public-sector corruption figures in the argument in which one of the following ways?

Point at Issue Question

A question that asks you to identify the specific claim, statement, or recommendation about which two speakers/authors disagree (or, rarely, about which they agree). Typical question stems:

> A point at issue between Tom and Jerry is

> The dialogue most strongly supports the claim that Marilyn and Billy disagree with each other about which one of the following?

Method of Argument Question

A question that asks you to describe an author's argumentative strategy. In other words, the correct answer describes *how* the author argues (not necessarily what the author says). Typical question stems:

> Which one of the following most accurately describes the technique of reasoning employed by the argument?

> Julian's argument proceeds by

> In the dialogue, Alexander responds to Abigail in which one of the following ways?

Parallel Reasoning Question

A question that asks you to identify the answer choice containing an argument that has the same logical structure and reaches the same type of conclusion as the argument in the stimulus does. Typical question stems:

> The pattern of reasoning in which one of the following arguments is most parallel to that in the argument above?

> The pattern of reasoning in which one of the following arguments is most similar to the pattern of reasoning in the argument above?

Assumption-Family Questions

Assumption Question

A question that asks you to identify one of the unstated premises in an author's argument. Assumption questions come in two varieties.

Necessary Assumption questions ask you to identify an unstated premise required for an argument's conclusion to follow logically from its evidence. Typical question stems:

> Which one of the following is an assumption on which the argument depends?

> Which one of the following is an assumption that the argument requires in order for its conclusion to be properly drawn?

Sufficient Assumption questions ask you to identify an unstated premise sufficient to establish the argument's conclusion on the basis of its evidence. Typical question stems:

> The conclusion follows logically if which one of the following is assumed?

> Which one of the following, if assumed, enables the conclusion above to be properly inferred?

Strengthen/Weaken Question

A question that asks you to identify a fact that, if true, would make the argument's conclusion more likely (Strengthen) or less likely (Weaken) to follow from its evidence. Typical question stems:

Strengthen

> Which one of the following, if true, most strengthens the argument above?

> Which one the following, if true, most strongly supports the claim above?

Weaken

Which one of the following, if true, would most weaken the argument above?

Which one of the following, if true, most calls into question the claim above?

Flaw Question

A question that asks you to describe the reasoning error that the author has made in an argument. Typical question stems:

The argument's reasoning is most vulnerable to criticism on the grounds that the argument

Which of the following identifies a reasoning error in the argument?

The reasoning in the correspondent's argument is questionable because the argument

Parallel Flaw Question

A question that asks you to identify the argument that contains the same error(s) in reasoning that the argument in the stimulus contains. Typical question stems:

The pattern of flawed reasoning exhibited by the argument above is most similar to that exhibited in which one of the following?

Which one of the following most closely parallels the questionable reasoning cited above?

Evaluate the Argument Question

A question that asks you to identify an issue or consideration relevant to the validity of an argument. Think of Evaluate questions as "Strengthen or Weaken" questions. The correct answer, if true, will strengthen the argument, and if false, will weaken the argument, or vice versa. Evaluate questions are very rare. Typical question stems:

Which one of the following would be most useful to know in order to evaluate the legitimacy of the professor's argument?

It would be most important to determine which one of the following in evaluating the argument?

Non-Argument Questions

Inference Question

A question that asks you to identify a statement that follows from the statements in the stimulus. It is very important to note the characteristics of the one correct and the four incorrect answers before evaluating the choices in Inference questions. Depending on the wording of the question stem,

the correct answer to an Inference question may be the one that

- *must be true* if the statements in the stimulus are true

- is *most strongly supported* by the statements in the stimulus

- *must be false* if the statements in the stimulus are true

Typical question stems:

If all of the statements above are true, then which one of the following must also be true?

Which one of the following can be properly inferred from the information above?

If the statements above are true, then each of the following could be true EXCEPT:

Which one of the following is most strongly supported by the information above?

The statements above, if true, most support which one of the following?

The facts described above provide the strongest evidence against which one of the following?

Paradox Question

A question that asks you to identify a fact that, if true, most helps to explain, resolve, or reconcile an apparent contradiction. Typical question stems:

Which one of the following, if true, most helps to explain how both studies' findings could be accurate?

Which one the following, if true, most helps to resolve the apparent conflict in the spokesperson's statements?

Each one of the following, if true, would contribute to an explanation of the apparent discrepancy in the information above EXCEPT:

Principle Questions

Principle Question

A question that asks you to identify corresponding cases and principles. Some Principle questions provide a principle in the stimulus and call for the answer choice describing a case that corresponds to the principle. Others provide a specific case in the stimulus and call for the answer containing a principle to which that case corresponds.

On the LSAT, Principle questions almost always mirror the skills rewarded by other Logical Reasoning question types. After each of the following Principle question stems, we note the question type it resembles. Typical question stems:

Which one of the following principles, if valid, most helps to justify the reasoning above? (**Strengthen**)

KAPLAN

Which one of the following most accurately expresses the principle underlying the reasoning above? (**Assumption**)

The situation described above most closely conforms to which of the following generalizations? (**Inference**)

Which one of the following situations conforms most closely to the principle described above? (**Inference**)

Which one of the following principles, if valid, most helps to reconcile the apparent conflict among the prosecutor's claims? (**Paradox**)

Parallel Principle Question

A question that asks you to identify a specific case that illustrates the same principle that is illustrated by the case described in the stimulus. Typical question stem:

Of the following, which one illustrates a principle that is most similar to the principle illustrated by the passage?

Untangling the Stimulus

Conclusion Types

The conclusions in arguments found in the Logical Reasoning section of the LSAT tend to fall into one of six categories:

1) Value Judgment (an evaluative statement; e.g., Action X is unethical, or Y's recital was poorly sung)

2) "If"/Then (a conditional prediction, recommendation, or assertion; e.g., If X is true, then so is Y, or If you an M, then you should do N)

3) Prediction (X *will* or *will not* happen in the future)

4) Comparison (X is taller/shorter/more common/less common, etc. than Y)

5) Assertion of Fact (X is true or X is false)

6) Recommendation (we *should* or *should not* do X)

One-Sentence Test

A tactic used to identify the author's conclusion in an argument. Consider which sentence in the argument is the one the author would keep if asked to get rid of everything except her main point.

Subsidiary Conclusion

A conclusion following from one piece of evidence and then used by the author to support his overall conclusion or main point. Consider the following argument:

The pharmaceutical company's new experimental treatment did not succeed in clinical trials. As a result, the new treatment will not reach the market this year. Thus,

the company will fall short of its revenue forecasts for the year.

Here, the sentence "As a result, the new treatment will not reach the market this year" is a subsidiary conclusion. It follows from the evidence that the new treatment failed in clinical trials, and it provides evidence for the overall conclusion that the company will not meet its revenue projections.

Keyword(s) in Logical Reasoning

A word or phrase that helps you untangle a question's stimulus by indicating the logical structure of the argument or the author's point. Here are three categories of Keywords to which LSAT experts pay special attention in Logical Reasoning:

Conclusion words; e.g., *therefore, thus, so, as a result, it follows that, consequently*, [evidence] *is evidence that* [conclusion]

Evidence word; e.g, *because, since, after all, for*, [evidence] *is evidence that* [conclusion]

Contrast words; e.g., *but, however, while, despite, in spite of, on the other hand* (These are especially useful in Paradox and Inference questions.)

Experts use Keywords even more extensively in Reading Comprehension. Learn the Keywords associated with the Reading Comprehension section, and apply them to Logical Reasoning when they are helpful.

Mismatched Concepts

One of two patterns to which authors' assumptions conform in LSAT arguments. Mismatched Concepts describes the assumption in arguments in which terms or concepts in the conclusion are different *in kind* from those in the evidence. The author assumes that there is a logical relationship between the different terms. For example:

Bobby is a **championship swimmer**. Therefore, he **trains every day**.

Here, the words "trains every day" appear only in the conclusion, and the words "championship swimmer" appear only in the evidence. For the author to reach this conclusion from this evidence, he assumes that championship swimmers train every day.

Another example:

Susan does **not eat her vegetables**. Thus, she will **not grow big and strong**.

In this argument, not growing big and strong is found only in the conclusion while not eating vegetables is found only in the evidence. For the author to reach this conclusion from this evidence, she must assume that eating one's vegetables is necessary for one to grow big and strong.

See also Overlooked Possibilities.

Overlooked Possibilities

One of two patterns to which authors' assumptions conform in LSAT arguments. Mismatched Concepts describes the assumption in arguments in which terms or concepts in the conclusion are different *in degree, scale, or level of certainty* from those in the evidence. The author assumes that there is no factor or explanation for the conclusion other than the one(s) offered in the evidence. For example:

> Samson does not have a ticket stub for this movie showing. Thus, Samson must have sneaked into the movie without paying.

The author assumes that there is no other explanation for Samson's lack of a ticket stub. The author overlooks several possibilities: e.g., Samson had a special pass for this showing of the movie; Samson dropped his ticket stub by accident or threw it away after entering the theater; someone else in Samson's party has all of the party members' ticket stubs in her pocket or handbag.

Another example:

> Jonah's marketing plan will save the company money. Therefore, the company should adopt Jonah's plan.

Here, the author makes a recommendation based on one advantage. The author assumes that the advantage is the company's only concern or that there are no disadvantages that could outweigh it, e.g., Jonah's plan might save money on marketing but not generate any new leads or customers; Jonah's plan might damage the company's image or reputation; Jonah's plan might include illegal false advertising. Whenever the author of an LSAT argument concludes with a recommendation or a prediction based on just a single fact in the evidence, that author is always overlooking many other possibilities.

See also Mismatched Concepts.

Causal Argument

An argument in which the author concludes or assumes that one thing causes another. The most common pattern on the LSAT is for the author to conclude that A causes B from evidence that A and B are correlated. For example:

> I notice that whenever the store has a poor sales month, employee tardiness is also higher that month. Therefore, it must be that employee tardiness causes the store to lose sales.

The author assumes that the correlation in the evidence indicates a causal relationship. These arguments are vulnerable to three types of overlooked possibilities:

1) There could be **another causal factor**. In the previous example, maybe the months in question are those in which the manager takes vacation, causing the store to lose sales and permitting employees to arrive late without fear of the boss's reprimands.

2) Causation could be **reversed**. Maybe in months when sales are down, employee morale suffers and tardiness increases as a result.

3) The correlation could be **coincidental**. Maybe the correlation between tardiness and the dip in sales is pure coincidence.

See also Flaw Types: Correlation versus Causation.

Another pattern in causal arguments (less frequent on the LSAT) involves the assumption that a particular causal mechanism is or is not involved in a causal relationship. For example:

> The airport has rerouted takeoffs and landings so that they will not create noise over the Sunnyside neighborhood. Thus, the recent drop in Sunnyside's property values cannot be explained by the neighborhood's proximity to the airport.

Here, the author assumes that the only way that the airport could be the cause of dropping property values is through noise pollution. The author overlooks any other possible mechanism (e.g., frequent traffic jams and congestion) through which proximity to the airport could be cause of Sunnyside's woes.

Principle

A broad, law-like rule, definition, or generalization that covers a variety of specific cases with defined attributes. To see how principles are treated on the LSAT, consider the following principle:

> It is immoral for a person for his own gain to mislead another person.

That principle would cover a specific case, such as a seller who lies about the quality of construction to get a higher price for his house. It would also correspond to the case of a teenager who, wishing to spend a night out on the town, tells his mom "I'm going over to Randy's house." He knows that his mom believes that he will be staying at Randy's house, when in fact, he and Randy will go out together.

That principle does not, however, cover cases in which someone lies solely for the purpose of making the other person feel better or in which one person inadvertently misleads the other through a mistake of fact.

Be careful not to apply your personal ethics or morals when analyzing the principles articulated on the test.

Flaw Types

Necessary versus Sufficient

This flaw occurs when a speaker or author concludes that one event is necessary for a second event from evidence that the first event is sufficient to bring about the second event, or vice versa. Example:

> If more than 25,000 users attempt to access the new app at the same time, the server will crash. Last night, at 11:15 PM, the server crashed, so it must be case that more than 25,000 users were attempting to use the new app at that time.

In making this argument, the author assumes that the only thing that will cause the server to crash is the usage level (i.e., high usage is *necessary* for the server to crash). The evidence, however, says that high usage is one thing that will cause the server to crash (i.e., that high usage is *sufficient* to crash the server).

Correlation versus Causation

This flaw occurs when a speaker or author draws a conclusion that one thing causes another from evidence that the two things are correlated. Example:

> Over the past half century, global sugar consumption has tripled. That same time period has seen a surge in the rate of technological advancement worldwide. It follows that the increase in sugar consumption has caused the acceleration in technological advancement.

In any argument with this structure, the author is making three unwarranted assumptions. First, he assumes that there is no alternate cause, i.e., there is nothing else that has contributed to rapid technological advancement. Second, he assumes that the causation is not reversed, i.e., technological advancement has not contributed to the increase in sugar consumption, perhaps by making it easier to grow, refine, or transport sugar. And, third, he assumes that the two phenomena are not merely coincidental, i.e., that it is not just happenstance that global sugar consumption is up at the same time that the pace of technological advancement has accelerated.

Unrepresentative Sample

This flaw occurs when a speaker or author draws a conclusion about a group from evidence in which the sample cannot represent that group because the sample is too small or too selective, or is biased in some way. Example:

> Moviegoers in our town prefer action films and romantic comedies over other film genres. Last Friday, we sent reporters to survey moviegoers at several theaters in town, and nearly 90 percent of those surveyed were going to watch either an action film or a romantic comedy.

The author assumes that the survey was representative of the town's moviegoers, but there are several reasons to question that assumption. First, we don't know how many people were actually surveyed. Even if the number of people surveyed was adequate, we don't know how many other types of movies were playing. Finally, the author doesn't limit her conclusion to moviegoers on Friday nights. If the survey had been conducted at Sunday matinees, maybe most moviegoers would have been heading out to see an animated family film or a historical drama. Who knows?

Scope Shift/Unwarranted Assumption

This flaw occurs when a speaker's or author's evidence has a scope or has terms different enough from the scope or terms in his conclusion that it is doubtful that the evidence can support the conclusion. Example:

> A very small percentage of working adults in this country can correctly define collateralized debt obligation securities. Thus, sad to say, the majority of the nation's working adults cannot make prudent choices about how to invest their savings.

This speaker assumes that prudent investing requires the ability to accurately define a somewhat obscure financial term. But prudence is not the same thing as expertise, and the speaker does not offer any evidence that this knowledge of this particular term is related to wise investing.

Percent versus Number/Rate versus Number

This flaw occurs when a speaker or author draws a conclusion about real quantities from evidence about rates or percentages, or vice versa. Example:

> At the end of last season, Camp SunnyDay laid off half of their senior counselors and a quarter of their junior counselors. Thus, Camp SunnyDay must have more senior counselors than junior counselors.

The problem, of course, is that we don't know how many senior and junior counselors were on staff before the layoffs. If there were a total of 4 senior counselors and 20 junior counselors, then the camp would have laid off only 2 senior counselors while dismissing 5 junior counselors.

Equivocation

This flaw occurs when a speaker or author uses the same word in two different and incompatible ways. Example:

> Our opponent in the race has accused our candidate's staff members of behaving unprofessionally. But that's not

fair. Our staff is made up entirely of volunteers, not paid campaign workers.

The speaker interprets the opponent's use of the word *professional* to mean "paid," but the opponent likely meant something more along the lines of "mature, competent, and businesslike."

Ad Hominem

This flaw occurs when a speaker or author concludes that another person's claim or argument is invalid because that other person has a personal flaw or shortcoming. One common pattern is for the speaker or author to claim the other person acts hypocritically or that the other person's claim is made from self-interest. Example:

> Mrs. Smithers testified before the city council, stating that the speed limits on the residential streets near her home are dangerously high. But why should we give her claim any credence? The way she eats and exercises, she's not even looking out for her own health.

The author attempts to undermine Mrs. Smithers's testimony by attacking her character and habits. He doesn't offer any evidence that is relevant to her claim about speed limits.

Part versus Whole

This flaw occurs when a speaker or author concludes that a part or individual has a certain characteristic because the whole or the larger group has that characteristic, or vice versa. Example:

> Patient: I should have no problems taking the three drugs prescribed to me by my doctors. I looked them up, and none of the three is listed as having any major side effects.

Here, the patient is assuming that what is true of each of the drugs individually will be true of them when taken together. The patient's flaw is overlooking possible interactions that could cause problems not present when the drugs are taken separately.

Circular Reasoning

This flaw occurs when a speaker or author tries to prove a conclusion with evidence that is logically equivalent to the conclusion. Example:

> All those who run for office are prevaricators. To   see this, just consider politicians: they all prevaricate.

Perhaps the author has tried to disguise the circular reasoning in this argument by exchanging the words "those who run for office" in the conclusion for "politicians" in the evidence, but all this argument amounts to is "Politicians prevaricate; therefore, politicians prevaricate." On the LSAT, circular

reasoning is very rarely the correct answer to a Flaw question, although it is regularly described in one of the wrong answers.

Question Strategies

Denial Test

A tactic for identifying the assumption *necessary* to an argument. When you negate an assumption necessary to an argument, the argument will fall apart. Negating an assumption that is not necessary to the argument will not invalidate the argument. Consider the following argument:

> Only high schools which produced a state champion athlete during the school year will be represented at the Governor's awards banquet. Therefore, McMurtry High School will be represented at the Governor's awards banquet.

Which one of the following is an assumption necessary to that argument?

> (1) McMurtry High School produced more state champion athletes than any other high school during the school year.

> (2) McMurtry High School produced at least one state champion athlete during the school year.

If you are at all confused about which of those two statements reflects the *necessary* assumption, negate them both.

> (1) McMurtry High School **did not produce more** state champion athletes than any other high school during the school year.

That does not invalidate the argument. McMurtry could still be represented at the Governor's banquet.

> (2) McMurtry High School **did not produce any** state champion athletes during the school year.

Here, negating the statement causes the argument to fall apart. Statement (2) is an assumption *necessary* to the argument.

Point at Issue "Decision Tree"

A tactic for evaluating the answer choices in Point at Issue questions. The correct answer is the only answer choice to which you can answer "Yes" to all three questions in the following diagram.

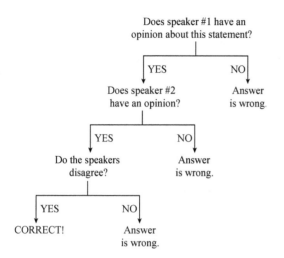

Common Methods of Argument

These methods of argument or argumentative strategies are common on the LSAT:

- Analogy, in which an author draws parallels between two unrelated (but purportedly similar) situations
- Example, in which an author cites a specific case or cases to justify a generalization
- Counterexample, in which an author seeks to discredit an opponent's argument by citing a specific case or cases that appear to invalidate the opponent's generalization
- Appeal to authority, in which an author cites an expert's claim or opinion as support for her conclusion
- Ad hominem attack, in which an author attacks her opponent's personal credibility rather than attacking the substance of her opponent's argument
- Elimination of alternatives, in which an author lists possibilities and discredits or rules out all but one
- Means/requirements, in which the author argues that something is needed to achieve a desired result

Wrong Answer Types in LR

Outside the Scope (Out of Scope; Beyond the Scope)

An answer choice containing a statement that is too broad, too narrow, or beyond the purview of the stimulus, making the statement in the choice irrelevant

180

An answer choice that directly contradicts what the correct answer must say (for example, a choice that strengthens the argument in a Weaken question)

Extreme

An answer choice containing language too emphatic to be supported by the stimulus; often (although not always) characterized by words such as *all*, *never*, *every*, *only*, or *most*

Distortion

An answer choice that mentions details from the stimulus but mangles or misstates what the author said about those details

Irrelevant Comparison

An answer choice that compares two items or attributes in a way not germane to the author's argument or statements

Half-Right/Half-Wrong

An answer choice that begins correctly, but then contradicts or distorts the passage in its second part; this wrong answer type is more common in Reading Comprehension than it is in Logical Reasoning

Faulty Use of Detail

An answer choice that accurately states something from the stimulus, but does so in a manner that answers the question incorrectly; this wrong answer type is more common in Reading Comprehension than it is in Logical Reasoning

Logic Games

Game Types

Strict Sequencing Game

A game that asks you to arrange entities into numbered positions or into a set schedule (usually hours or days). Strict Sequencing is, by far, the most common game type on the LSAT. In the typical Strict Sequencing game, there is a one-to-one matchup of entities and positions, e.g., seven entities to be placed in seven positions, one per position, or six entities to be placed over six consecutive days, one entity per day.

From time to time, the LSAT will offer Strict Sequencing with more entities than positions (e.g., seven entities to be arranged over five days, with some days to receive more than one entity) or more positions than entities (e.g., six entities to be scheduled over seven days, with at least one day to receive no entities).

Other, less common variations on Strict Sequencing include:

Double Sequencing, in which each entity is placed or scheduled two times (there have been rare occurrences of Triple or Quadruple Sequencing). Alternatively, a Double Sequencing game may involve two different sets of entities each sequenced once.

Circular Sequencing, in which entities are arranged around a table or in a circular arrangement (NOTE: When the positions in a Circular Sequencing game are numbered, the first and last positions are adjacent.)

Vertical Sequencing, in which the positions are numbered from top to bottom or from bottom to top (as in the floors of a building)

Loose Sequencing Game

A game that asks you to arrange or schedule entities in order but provides no numbering or naming of the positions. The rules in Loose Sequencing give only the relative positions (earlier or later, higher or lower) between two entities or among three entities. Loose Sequencing games almost always provide that there will be no ties between entities in the rank, order, or position they take.

Circular Sequencing Game

See Strict Sequencing Game.

Selection Game

A game that asks you to choose or include some entities from the initial list of entities and to reject or exclude others. Some Selection games provide overall limitations on the number of entities to be selected (e.g., "choose exactly four of seven students" or "choose at least two of six entrees") while others provide little or no restriction on the number selected ("choose at least one type of flower" or "select from among seven board members").

Distribution Game

A game that asks you to break up the initial list of entities into two, three, or (very rarely) four groups or teams. In the vast majority of Distribution games, each entity is assigned to one and only one group or team. A relatively common variation on Distribution games will provide a subdivided list of entities (e.g., eight students—four men and four women—will form three study groups) and will then require representatives from those subdivisions on each team (e.g., each study group will have at least one of the men on it).

Matching Game

A game that asks you to match one or more members of one set of entities to specific members of another set of entities, or that asks you to match attributes or objects to a set of entities. Unlike Distribution games, in which each entity is placed in exactly one group or team, Matching games usually permit you to assign the same attribute or object to more than one entity.

In some cases, there are overall limitations on the number of entities that can be matched (e.g., "In a school's wood shop, there are four workstations—numbered 1 through 4—and each workstation has at least one and at most three of the following tools—band saw, dremmel tool, electric sander, and power drill"). In almost all Matching games, further restrictions on the number of entities that can be matched to a particular person or place will be found in the rules (e.g., Workstation 4 will have more tools than Workstation 2 has).

Hybrid Game

A game that asks you to do two (or rarely, three) of the standard actions (Sequencing, Selection, Distribution, and Matching) to a set of entities.

The most common Hybrid is Sequencing-Matching. A typical Sequencing-Matching Hybrid game might ask you to schedule six speakers at a conference to six one-hour speaking slots (from 9 AM to 2 PM), and then assign each speaker one of two subjects (economic development or trade policy).

Nearly as common as Sequencing-Matching is Distribution-Sequencing. A typical game of this type might ask you to divide six people in a talent competition into either a Dance category or a Singing category, and then rank the competitors in each category.

It is most common to see one Hybrid game in each Logic Games section, although there have been tests with two Hybrid games and tests with none. To determine the type of Hybrid you are faced with, identify the game's action in Step 1 of the Logic Games Method. For example, a game asking you to choose four of six runners, and then assign the four chosen runners to lanes numbered 1 through 4 on a track, would be a Selection-Sequencing Hybrid game.

Mapping Game

A game that provides you with a description of geographical locations and, typically, of the connections among them. Mapping games often ask you to determine the shortest possible routes between two locations or to account for the number of connections required to travel from one location to another. This game type is extremely rare, and as of February 2017, a Mapping game was last seen on PrepTest 40 administered in June 2003.

Process Game

A game that opens with an initial arrangement of entities (e.g., a starting sequence or grouping) and provides rules that describe the processes through which that arrangement can be altered. The questions typically ask you for acceptable arrangements or placements of particular entities after one, two, or three stages in the process. Occasionally, a Process game question might provide information about the arrangement after one, two, or three stages in the process and ask you what must have happened in the earlier stages. This game type is extremely rare, and as of November 2016, a Process game was last seen on PrepTest 16 administered in September 1995. However, there was a Process game on PrepTest 80, administered in December 2016, thus ending a 20-year hiatus.

Game Setups and Deductions

Floater

An entity that is not restricted by any rule or limitation in the game

Blocks of Entities

Two or more entities that are required by rule to be adjacent or separated by a set number of spaces (Sequencing games), to be placed together in the same group (Distribution games), to be matched to the same entity (Matching games), or to be selected or rejected together (Selection games)

Limited Options

Rules or restrictions that force all of a game's acceptable arrangements into two (or occasionally three) patterns

Established Entities

An entity required by rule to be placed in one space or assigned to one particular group throughout the entire game

Number Restrictions

Rules or limitations affecting the number of entities that may be placed into a group or space throughout the game

Duplications

Two or more rules that restrict a common entity. Usually, these rules can be combined to reach additional deductions. For example, if you know that B is placed earlier than A in a sequence and that C is placed earlier than B in that sequence, you can deduce that C is placed earlier than A in the sequence

and that there is at least one space (the space occupied by B) between C and A.

Master Sketch

The final sketch derived from the game's setup, rules, and deductions. LSAT experts preserve the Master Sketch for reference as they work through the questions. The Master Sketch does not include any conditions from New-"If" question stems.

Logic Games Question Types

Acceptability Question

A question in which the correct answer is an acceptable arrangement of all the entities relative to the spaces, groups, or selection criteria in the game. Answer these by using the rules to eliminate answer choices that violate the rules.

Partial Acceptability Question

A question in which the correct answer is an acceptable arrangement of some of the entities relative to some of the spaces, groups, or selection criteria in the game, and in which the arrangement of entities not included in the answer choices could be acceptable to the spaces, groups, or selection criteria not explicitly shown in the answer choices. Answer these the same way you would answer Acceptability questions, by using the rules to eliminate answer choices that explicitly or implicitly violate the rules.

Must Be True/False; Could Be True/False Question

A question in which the correct answer must be true, could be true, could be false, or must be false (depending on the question stem), and in which no additional rules or conditions are provided by the question stem

New-"If" Question

A question in which the stem provides an additional rule, condition, or restriction (applicable only to that question), and then asks what must/could be true/false as a result. LSAT experts typically handle New-"If" questions by copying the Master Sketch, adding the new restriction to the copy, and working out any additional deductions available as a result of the new restriction before evaluating the answer choices.

Rule Substitution Question

A question in which the correct answer is a rule that would have an impact identical to one of the game's original rules on the entities in the game

Rule Change Question

A question in which the stem alters one of the original rules in the game, and then asks what must/could be true/false as a result. LSAT experts typically handle Rule Change questions by reconstructing the game's sketch, but now accounting for the changed rule in place of the original. These questions are rare on recent tests.

Rule Suspension Question

A question in which the stem indicates that you should ignore one of the original rules in the game, and then asks what must/could be true/false as a result. LSAT experts typically handle Rule Suspension questions by reconstructing the game's sketch, but now accounting for the absent rule. These questions are very rare.

Complete and Accurate List Question

A question in which the correct answer is a list of any and all entities that could acceptably appear in a particular space or group, or a list of any and all spaces or groups in which a particular entity could appear

Completely Determine Question

A question in which the correct answer is a condition that would result in exactly one acceptable arrangement for all of the entities in the game

Supply the "If" Question

A question in which the correct answer is a condition that would guarantee a particular result stipulated in the question stem

Minimum/Maximum Question

A question in which the correct answer is the number corresponding to the fewest or greatest number of entities that could be selected (Selection), placed into a particular group (Distribution), or matched to a particular entity (Matching). Often, Minimum/Maximum questions begin with New-"If" conditions.

Earliest/Latest Question

A question in which the correct answer is the earliest or latest position in which an entity may acceptably be placed. Often, Earliest/Latest questions begin with New-"If" conditions.

"How Many" Question

A question in which the correct answer is the exact number of entities that may acceptably be placed into a particular group

or space. Often, "How Many" questions begin with New-"If" conditions.

Reading Comprehension

Strategic Reading

Roadmap

The test taker's markup of the passage text in Step 1 (Read the Passage Strategically) of the Reading Comprehension Method. To create helpful Roadmaps, LSAT experts circle or underline Keywords in the passage text and jot down brief, helpful notes or paragraph summaries in the margin of their test booklets.

Keyword(s) in Reading Comprehension

Words in the passage text that reveal the passage structure or the author's point of view and thus help test takers anticipate and research the questions that accompany the passage. LSAT experts pay attention to six categories of Keywords in Reading Comprehension:

Emphasis/Opinion—words that signal that the author finds a detail noteworthy or that the author has positive or negative opinion about a detail; any subjective or evaluative language on the author's part (e.g., *especially*, *crucial*, *unfortunately*, *disappointing*, *I suggest*, *it seems likely*)

Contrast—words indicating that the author finds two details or ideas incompatible or that the two details illustrate conflicting points (e.g., *but*, *yet*, *despite*, *on the other hand*)

Logic—words that indicate an argument, either the author's or someone else's (e.g., *thus*, *therefore*, *because*, *it follows that*)

Illustration—words indicating an example offered to clarify or support another point (e.g., *for example*, *this shows*, *to illustrate*)

Sequence/Chronology—words showing steps in a process or developments over time (e.g., *traditionally*, *in the past*, *today*, *first*, *second*, *finally*, *earlier*, *subsequent*)

Continuation—words indicating that a subsequent example or detail supports the same point or illustrates the same idea as the previous example (e.g., *moreover*, *in addition*, *also*, *further*, *along the same lines*)

Margin Notes

The brief notes or paragraph summaries that the test taker jots down next to the passage in the margin of the test booklet

Big Picture Summaries: Topic/Scope/Purpose/Main Idea

A test taker's mental summary of the passage as a whole made during Step 1 (Read the Passage Strategically) of the

Reading Comprehension Method. LSAT experts account for four aspects of the passage in their big picture summaries:

Topic—the overall subject of the passage

Scope—the particular aspect of the Topic that the author focuses on

Purpose—the author's reason or motive for writing the passage (express this as a verb; e.g., *to refute*, *to outline*, *to evaluate*, *to critique*)

Main Idea—the author's conclusion or overall takeaway; if the passage does not contain an explicit conclusion or thesis, you can combine the author's Scope and Purpose to get a good sense of the Main Idea.

Passage Types

Kaplan categorizes Reading Comprehension passages in two ways, by subject matter and by passage structure.

Subject matter categories

In the majority of LSAT Reading Comprehension sections, there is one passage from each of the following subject matter categories:

Humanities—topics from art, music, literature, philosophy, etc.

Natural Science—topics from biology, astronomy, paleontology, physics, etc.

Social Science—topics from anthropology, history, sociology, psychology, etc.

Law—topics from constitutional law, international law, legal education, jurisprudence, etc.

Passage structure categories

The majority of LSAT Reading Comprehension passages correspond to one of the following descriptions. The first categories—Theory/Perspective and Event/Phenomenon—have been the most common on recent LSATs.

Theory/Perspective—The passage focuses on a thinker's theory or perspective on some aspect of the Topic; typically (though not always), the author disagrees and critiques the thinker's perspective and/or defends his own perspective.

Event/Phenomenon—The passage focuses on an event, a breakthrough development, or a problem that has recently arisen; when a solution to the problem is proposed, the author most often agrees with the solution (and that represents the passage's Main Idea).

Biography—The passage discusses something about a notable person; the aspect of the person's life emphasized by the author reflects the Scope of the passage.

Debate—The passage outlines two opposing positions (neither of which is the author's) on some aspect of the Topic; the author may side with one of the positions, may remain neutral, or may critique both. (This structure has been relatively rare on recent LSATs.)

Comparative Reading

A pair of passages (labeled Passage A and Passage B) that stand in place of the typical single passage exactly one time in each Reading Comprehension section administered since June 2007. The paired Comparative Reading passages share the same Topic, but may have different Scopes and Purposes. On most LSAT tests, a majority of the questions accompanying Comparative Reading passages require the test taker to compare or contrast ideas or details from both passages.

Question Strategies

Research Clues

A reference in a Reading Comprehension question stem to a word, phrase, or detail in the passage text, or to a particular line number or paragraph in the passage. LSAT experts recognize five kinds of research clues:

Line Reference—An LSAT expert researches around the referenced lines, looking for Keywords that indicate why the referenced details were included or how they were used by the author.

Paragraph Reference—An LSAT expert consults her passage Roadmap to see the paragraph's Scope and Purpose.

Quoted Text (often accompanied by a line reference)—An LSAT expert checks the context of the quoted term or phrase, asking what the author meant by it in the passage.

Proper Nouns—An LSAT expert checks the context of the person, place, or thing in the passage, asking whether the author made a positive, negative, or neutral evaluation of it and why the author included it in the passage.

Content Clues—These are terms, concepts, or ideas from the passage mentioned in the question stem but not as direct quotes and not accompanied by line references. An LSAT expert knows that content clues almost always refer to something that the author emphasized or about which the author expressed an opinion.

Reading Comp Question Types

Global Question

A question that asks for the Main Idea of the passage or for the author's primary Purpose in writing the passage. Typical question stems:

> Which one of the following most accurately expresses the main point of the passage?

The primary purpose of the passage is to

Detail Question

A question that asks what the passage explicitly states about a detail. Typical question stems:

> According to the passage, some critics have criticized Gilliam's films on the grounds that

> The passage states that one role of a municipality's comptroller in budget decisions by the city council is to

> The author identifies which one of the following as a commonly held but false preconception?

> The passage contains sufficient information to answer which of the following questions?

Occasionally, the test will ask for a correct answer that contains a detail *not* stated in the passage:

> The author attributes each of the following positions to the Federalists EXCEPT:

Inference Question

A question that asks for a statement that follows from or is based on the passage but that is not necessarily stated explicitly in the passage. Some Inference questions contain research clues. The following are typical Inference question stems containing research clues:

> Based on the passage, the author would be most likely to agree with which one of the following statements about unified field theory?

> The passage suggests which one of the following about the behavior of migratory water fowl?

> Given the information in the passage, to which one of the following would radiocarbon dating techniques likely be applicable?

Other Inference questions lack research clues in the question stem. They may be evaluated using the test taker's Big Picture Summaries, or the answer choices may make it clear that the test taker should research a particular part of the passage text. The following are typical Inference question stems containing research clues:

> It can be inferred from the passage that the author would be most likely to agree that

> Which one of the following statements is most strongly supported by the passage?

Other Reading Comprehension question types categorized as Inference questions are Author's Attitude questions and Vocabulary-in-Context questions.

Logic Function Question

A question that asks why the author included a particular detail or reference in the passage or how the author used a particular detail or reference. Typical question stems:

> The author of the passage mentions declining inner-city populations in the paragraph most likely in order to

> The author's discussion of Rimbaud's travels in the Mediterranean (lines 23–28) functions primarily to

> Which one of the following best expresses the function of the third paragraph in the passage?

Logic Reasoning Question

A question that asks the test taker to apply Logical Reasoning skills in relation to a Reading Comprehension passage. Logic Reasoning questions often mirror Strengthen or Parallel Reasoning questions, and occasionally mirror Method of Argument or Principle questions. Typical question stems:

> Which one of the following, if true, would most strengthen the claim made by the author in the last sentence of the passage (lines 51–55)?

> Which one of the following pairs of proposals is most closely analogous to the pair of studies discussed in the passage?

Author's Attitude Question

A question that asks for the author's opinion or point of view on the subject discussed in the passage or on a detail mentioned in the passage. Since the correct answer may follow from the passage without being explicitly stated in it, some Author's Attitude questions are characterized as a subset of Inference questions. Typical question stems:

> The author's attitude toward the use of DNA evidence in the appeals by convicted felons is most accurately described as

> The author's stance regarding monetarist economic theories can most accurately be described as one of

Vocabulary-in-Context Question

A question that asks how the author uses a word or phrase within the context of the passage. The word or phrase in question is always one with multiple meanings. Since the correct answer follows from its use in the passage, Vocabulary-in-Context questions are characterized as a subset of Inference questions. Typical question stems:

> Which one of the following is closest in meaning to the word "citation" as it used in the second paragraph of the passage (line 18)?

> In context, the word "enlightenment" (line 24) refers to

Wrong Answer Types in RC

Outside the Scope (Out of Scope; Beyond the Scope)

An answer choice containing a statement that is too broad, too narrow, or beyond the purview of the passage

180

An answer choice that directly contradicts what the correct answer must say

Extreme

An answer choice containing language too emphatic (e.g., *all*, *never*, *every*, *none*) to be supported by the passage

Distortion

An answer choice that mentions details or ideas from the passage but mangles or misstates what the author said about those details or ideas

Faulty Use of Detail

An answer choice that accurately states something from the passage but in a manner that incorrectly answers the question

Half-Right/Half-Wrong

An answer choice in which one clause follows from the passage while another clause contradicts or deviates from the passage

Formal Logic Terms

Conditional Statement ("If"-Then Statement)

A statement containing a sufficient clause and a necessary clause. Conditional statements can be described in Formal Logic shorthand as:

If [sufficient clause] → [necessary clause]

In some explanations, the LSAT expert may refer to the sufficient clause as the statement's "trigger" and to the necessary clause as the statement's result.

For more on how to interpret, describe, and use conditional statements on the LSAT, please refer to "A Note About Formal Logic on the LSAT" in this book's introduction.

Contrapositive

The conditional statement logically equivalent to another conditional statement formed by reversing the order of and negating the terms in the original conditional statement. For example, reversing and negating the terms in this statement:

If	*A*	→	*B*

results in its contrapositive:

If	*~B*	→	*~A*

To form the contrapositive of conditional statements in which either the sufficient clause or the necessary clause has more than one term, you must also change the conjunction *and* to *or*, or vice versa. For example, reversing and negating the terms and changing *and* to *or* in this statement:

If	*M*	→	*O AND P*

results in its contrapositive:

If	*~O OR ~P*	→	*~M*

Printed in the USA
CPSIA information can be obtained
at www.ICGtesting.com
LVHW071000301223
767793LV00064B/4356